MANAGE *i*T

Version 1, Release 1

NEAL PATTERSON

This book was published by Cerner Corporation.
2800 Rockcreek Parkway,
Kansas City, MO 64117-2551

First Printing: May 2005

ISBN: 0-9765264-0-9
LCCN: 2005920180
Doc ID: 00FM00001

Book designed by

To Dad, who taught me my first lesson of business:

"Success follows hard work!"

Contents

Table of Figures

Foreword by Cliff Illig,
Cofounder, Cerner Corporation

Manage *i*T

I have known Neal Patterson for 32 years. We have been friends for 31 years. We have been colleagues and collaborators for 30 years. We have been business partners and cofounders of an enterprise for 25 years. As co-conspirators in small and grand endeavors for as long as I can remember, we have been trying to figure out what it means to manage from the very beginning.

If you are reading this book, you are most likely a Cerner associate facing the challenge of being a manager in a high-innovation, high-growth, high-performance company. You understand that much is expected of you. You recognize that, regardless of the size of your team, you have a great deal of responsibility, and with responsibility comes accountability. You face a daunting list: clients to satisfy, commitments to meet, milestones to achieve, architecture to uphold and enhance, new things to start, and work-in-process to finish. You must make peace between conflicting priorities, balance the demand for new commitments against your capacity to deliver, coordinate with others who do not share your priorities, and constantly sell what you and your team are doing. Through this all, the omnipresent challenge is to manage people.

My expectation is that if you have been at Cerner for any time at all, you are caught up in Cerner's vision and mission. You understand that what we do is unbelievably important. You understand that if we are successful, we can have a meaningful impact on the quality of millions of lives around the globe. We can significantly influence the micro and macro economics of healthcare and managing health, even to the point of making a measurable difference to entire nations. If you have been here, you also have this gnawing sensation that achieving our potential as an enterprise depends heavily on the quality of our managers and how skillfully they play their roles. Finally, you realize that "our managers" is *you*!

As a Cerner manager, Neal has written this book for *you*. It is Neal, our chief manager, sharing with all of us the results of 30 years of managing. This is not a book about management theory. This is a practicum. Because I share the long view of everything that has happened at Cerner, I can tell you that the values, principles, philosophies, beliefs, experience, discipline, tools, technique, and know-how that Neal has built into these pages are the real deal. So many of the lessons here are lessons I watched *grow* out of our daily experiences over nearly three decades. I promise you that there are several highly entertaining stories that support every chapter, page, and point in this book. Although some may label this "Version 1, Release 1," the contents of *Manage iT* are far beyond alpha or even beta quality code. This is the stuff that Neal has developed, learned, and used to build Cerner. This is the battle-tested stuff of real managers with really big jobs to do.

Over the years, I and others have encouraged Neal to *write it down*. We recognized that as we have continued to build our team, there is cumulative and incremental value we derive from the consistent application of sage and seasoned management approaches to our challenges at Cerner. We have an approach. When we follow it, the approach works. Unlike the many other very valuable books that suggest a one-size-fits-all approach to managing businesses of all stripes, the contents of this volume are highly relevant to the business and management environment we deal with every day. This is not just Neal's book about managing, this is Neal's book about managing Cerner.

I would suggest that when you read *Manage i*T the first time, you read it from start to finish. After that, use *i*T as a reference. Check *i*T. Talk about *i*T with your peers. Challenge *i*T. Share *i*Ts lessons with your team. Use *i*T to tune up your personal management style. Burn *i*T in. Having been the beneficiary of an incredibly productive partnership with Neal for so many years, I would encourage you to use his investment in *Manage i*T to form your own partnership of highly capable Cerner managers.

A final word. Find herein Neal's thoughtful lessons about the subject of management. These are not his lessons about how to build a large-scale software enterprise. They are not his lessons on leadership or entrepreneurship. If we make good use of *Manage i*T to create the best future for Cerner, I'm sure we will have his books with these other lessons to look forward to.

Cliff Illig
Cerner Cofounder

Acknowledgements

This book is a collection of thoughts I recorded over a number of years and put into this format during the summers of 2003 and 2004. Many of these thoughts were freely borrowed from books, people, and events that influenced me at the time I originally recorded them. Where my memory permits, I have tried to give proper credit. The truth is that thousands of people have contributed to the content of this book. Clients, associates, business partners, friends, mentors—each and every one has taught me something that has shaped my view of managing. But none has influenced me more so than my two partners in starting Cerner, Cliff Illig and Paul Gorup. Each awes me with a genius I have not seen in other people. Due to title and circumstance, I get too much of the credit for Cerner. Their contributions have been—and continue to be—immeasurable.

A number of my associates gave their valuable time and intellect to improving my manuscript through criticism or craft. Among those who left a mark on this book are Brad Allen, Paul Black, Renée Cozad, David Edwards, Kelly Lolli, Glen Martin, Clay Patterson, Eric Siley, Maria Stecklein, Jeff Townsend, and Julie Wilson. They each made valuable contributions to the material and should get credit. The mistakes still in the book, however, are my doing.

My family allows me my reclusive ways, which included several weeks alone at the lake to write the largest portions of this material. Both Amanda Hurd and Diane Rowell were my partners in scheduling enough time to write this book. And April Martin, my "angel" who appeared to me in written words and thoughts, not only unraveled my reflections, but made them coherent to future readers as well. To all, my thanks and gratitude.

Introduction

Manage *i*T

Managers manage.
To manage is to plan, execute, and control.
Managers manage people, projects, processes, and property.
That is about iT!

The title of this book is *Manage i*T. Some people see the word *manage* and think of a passive pursuit. When you see the word *manage* in this book, however, I want you to think of a dynamic verb; an aggressive, energetic, even physical activity—because when it is done properly, management is a full-contact sport. But what about *i*T? Those of you who have participated in the *Get IT* exchange in the past already know that I have a bit of an obsession with the word *it*, and I tend to use the word to mean a number of different things. In the context of management, however, *i*T has a specific meaning, one I have tried to reflect in spelling. Not only is management a full-contact sport, but it is also a team sport. The small "*i*" is you, the manager. The big "T" is the team. The sooner you realize this, the better.

This is a book for Cerner *managers only*. You, the intended reader, are a Cerner associate at the team lead level or higher. This book contains my personal philosophy, principles, and beliefs about the art of management, spiced with some Cerner history. I have lived the history, but I am no authority on the subject of management. I have never considered management to be my strong suit. In truth, I'd feel more competent writing about entrepreneurship, healthcare information technology, or even leadership—and indeed, some might wonder why my first book isn't devoted to one of my better-known passions. Not many people get an opportunity to start a successful business, and very few get an opportunity to grow a startup company to one with $1 billion in revenues. Still fewer get the chance to stand at the helm of an organization whose associates collectively pursue a task as meaningful or complex as improving healthcare. After more than thirty years of experience in business, and most of that in a leadership position at Cerner, I have come to hold some strong ideas about management. At this time in our company's history, I want to share my thoughts with you, manager to manager. Strong management is essential as we pursue our vision together of how to thrive both as a large, well run company and one that gives voice to the freedom and innovation that are part of our DNA.

As we start our second 25 years in 2005, Cerner has more than 6,000 associates operating in more than 20 countries. We have become a management team that is stretched around the world. It is getting more difficult to communicate even basic messages to the nearly 1,000 Cerner managers who share responsibility for leading our thoughts and actions each day. I will never know many of you, nor work with you closely, and yet we must accomplish great things together. How we manage will greatly affect the magnitude of our impact on healthcare, and will determine whether we reach our full potential as a company. Being a competent manager is a vital skill for every Cerner associate who is charged with the leadership of people, projects, processes, or property—from the front-line team leader with four direct reports—to the executive responsible for two-thirds of the company—to the CEO.

I wrote this book because you are on my team. Whether you are in the cubicle next door or an office halfway around the globe, you and I are in the same chain of command that connects all of our associates into one organization. I am the Chairman and CEO of Cerner, you work for me, and there are some concepts and ideas about management that I want to share with you. You will rarely hear me speak in such direct terms about the employer-employee relationship. Like many people, I do not naturally care for organizations that depend on hierarchical authority to get things done. If it were always possible for us to come together and achieve great things simply on the basis of knowing and respecting one another, having access to the same information, sharing a vision of the future, and agreeing about the best way to pursue it, then that is the way I'd prefer it. Most of our best moments as a company have come from exactly these types of interactions. The special caliber of relationship capable of achieving this level of unity, however, takes time to develop. Frequently, as you likely know from your own experiences as a manager, you will encounter less ideal conditions. Even on the smallest of teams, it is common for people to differ greatly from one another with regard to how well they know their managers and each of their coworkers, how much information they have access to, why they come to work in the morning, and what things they think should be done. Some people have a sense of the big picture; others do not. As managers of such teams, we have the responsibility to do everything we can to win our associates over, to earn their respect and trust, to share information, to tell them the why, and to help every member of our teams "get *i*T." While we are doing that (and it is a continual process), we also have to make sure the job still gets done. We have to set expectations. This book is a medium for me to do all of these things in my job as a manager—communicate and set expectations, coordinate across our growing and increasingly virtual management team, and work on developing less experienced associates into great leaders and managers.

NEAL PATTERSON

*Manage i*T is my pointed appeal to each of you to take your duty to serve Cerner associates seriously. There is a strength that comes from our chain of command, but there is also an implied weakness. Any time one of us as a manager fails to achieve part of our plan, does not deliver on a commitment, or breaks the trust with an associate, it harms every associate beneath the broken link in the chain of command. As CEO, if I am at fault, then it will affect our entire organization. Each of us has an awesome responsibility to the associates on our teams and, by extension, to all associates and clients.

In this book, I attempt to communicate broadly, yet intimately. I choose to communicate in the first and second person (*I* and *you*) wherever possible, because I do not intend to disguise this as an academic, authoritative management book. I assure you that there is no research behind these words, just 30 years of practical experience, some of it relevant. These are my thoughts, beliefs, and expectations. I want to share them with you. Only you will know if the contents of this book can help you become a more effective manager. *Manage i*T is not a formula. Many times my messages will not be on target for your specific situation. We both, however, have had to deal with clients, competitors, associates, intellectual property, and technology. On some occasions, the insights from my experience might contribute to your success. You will discover from reading this book that I have been on a lifetime journey to master the subject of management, and I am no master yet. It is my hope that this book will challenge you to *think* about where you are on your own journey—and then *act* to become a better manager.

Many topics are outside of the scope of this book. The book's fundamental point of view is from manager to manager. It does not attempt to represent the point of view of the person being managed. It will not coach you through what to do if you have a bad manager. This void may frustrate you if you see a definite weakness in your immediate manager. The truth is that this type of issue usually must be dealt with from above. Your view of your manager is extremely important and must become part of our management and measurement system. In connection with the first publishing of this book, I have asked that we reinstate Cerner's previous practice of conducting annual 360-degree reviews, through which all managers are evaluated not just by their immediate managers, but also by their peers and the associates who work directly for them.

I have said that this is not an authoritative book. If you are interested in other perspectives on management, there are plenty to be found. Methods of management have been devised for centuries, and new books about management are being written each month. Many say our current form of hierarchical management can be traced back to early China. The 5th-century B.C. Chinese general Sun Tzu recorded his thoughts on managing battles, wars, armies, and conquered countries in the book *The Art of War*, which I highly recommend. As our society entered the age of machines, the management of organizations became a much more studied subject. Frederick Taylor's essays and thoughts were published in the book *The Principles of Scientific Management* in 1911. Two years later, Henry Ford took Taylor's ideas and began building cars on a moving assembly line, a great innovation of the industrial age. No longer were our work efforts about individual craftsmanship; instead, we aggregated into enterprises and corporations designed to create value on a massive scale.

Peter Drucker is considered the father of the modern science of management. He was the first person to identify the emergence of a true knowledge organization with the knowledge worker at its center. Drucker is a prolific writer, and I have found pearls in each of his works that I have read. I had the privilege of meeting him in a small study group in 1998. He was everything that I had envisioned and more. If you can read only one of his books, I recommend *The Essential Drucker*.

Management theories aside, however, no other teachings summarize my beliefs about management as do the declarative statements I made at the outset: "Managers manage" and "To manage is to plan, execute, and control." The rest is detail.

Chapter One

You as the Manager— To Be, or Not To Be?

Look within!...The secret is inside you.
— Hui-neng

Managers manage. They manage people and things—processes, projects, and property. They must be intelligent, talented, skilled, motivated, and capable of operating under pressure. They are accountable to create business results that, in turn, create value for clients and shareholders. At Cerner, managers must be confident in their ability to create the transformed healthcare system in partnership with our clients, and they must possess the business skills to grow profits and generate the positive cash flow that fuels our future and demonstrates that our shareholders' trust in us is not misplaced.

But where do managers come from? How is a manager created? Some people plan for a career in management. For others, management sneaks up on them—perhaps as a consequence of doing well in a given role. At some point, regardless of the beginning, the same basic event occurs: a person— in this case, *you*—questions whether management is the desirable path.

Parents naturally set high expectations for their children, many times implying they should strive to attain positions of power and authority. I tell Cortney, my youngest daughter, that I believe she will be the first woman president of the United States. Early in life, we get signals that success is at least partially defined by being in charge. In reality, being in charge is not right for everyone and is not the only way to be highly successful. Many Cerner associates want to excel at things other than managing people or things.

The Difference Between *Managers* and *Leaders, Executives, & Entrepreneurs*

In the interest of clarity, I want to take a brief detour to share with you how I think a manager differs from a leader, an executive, or an entrepreneur. Frequently, two or more of these terms apply to the same person and role, making it hard to understand the subtle differences between descriptors. For practical but confusing illustrative purposes, I may be an example of all four. The labels are not always interchangeable, however, and I think it's important for you to know what I mean when I use the word *manager* throughout this book.

Manager vs. Leader

Managers manage. Leaders lead. It is almost impossible to write a book about management without also addressing the topic of leadership. Although the nouns *manager* and *leader* are used almost interchangeably (even by me), I do not consider them to be one and the same. The very best managers *also* are gifted leaders. Your manager is defined by the organization chart. Be assured that there is no "chart of leaders."

Cerner's future depends on being an organization of great leaders. Cerner was never intended to be a "lifestyle company" for myself or for anyone else. It is of vital importance that we develop a leadership culture inside Cerner that transcends individual leaders and their styles. This kind of culture will take the company into the next 50 years and beyond. We must be very careful to reward leadership, even when it does not equate to management.

What is a leader? I have already said being a leader is not the same thing as being a manager. The definition I have used for a very long time is that *a leader is someone whom others **voluntarily** follow*. In contemplating leadership, then, it is most interesting to ask why people in an organization follow someone. Below are some reasons I believe they do:

- *Because the person has a compelling vision*. One of the most powerful leadership skills is the ability to energetically describe a relevant future state—vision—that others value and are willing to commit themselves to achieving. If you describe a future that others want, you are leading.

- *Because the person is extraordinarily competent*. If you are really good at something, others listen and accept your ideas because they know you are competent. When all eyes go to you in a discussion to see whether you nod in approval, you are leading.

- *Because the person has uncompromising integrity*. If others know you have uncompromising integrity, they will trust you and accept the motivations behind your actions and ideas. They will follow you.

Vision, competency, and uncompromising integrity are at the center of what I believe makes for a great leader. Cerner needs to be a company of leaders. We have a very important role in our society—we need to transform healthcare. This will require great leadership from all of us. True leadership is totally independent of a person's title and position within an organization. I typically find that people follow others voluntarily for the reasons I listed above—the more of these qualities present, the stronger the inclination to follow. The qualifier _voluntarily_, however, begs a description of the final reason why people in an organization follow someone:

> • _Because the person is the boss._ I do not consider this leadership; I call it management. Management is a necessary part of executing a plan within an organization. Business organizations such as Cerner are not democracies; we do not vote. We must have a structure, ultimately hierarchical in nature, in which our management team has the authority to make and enforce decisions that keep us moving in a common direction.

As a manager, you will ask people to follow you before you get the chance to demonstrate your vision, competency, and integrity. _It is precisely because of the unearned weight of this authority that you must learn good and responsible management skills._

Manager vs. Executive

Executives must be good managers. I differentiate their abilities based on one additional skill, their ability to begin at the end. Managers are talented at getting from point A to point B. They start from where they are at a point in time and develop a plan to go where someone else—an executive—tells them. Executives start by thinking of where they want to be at some point in the future. Executives have a skill and habit to start at the end, envision their organization with the mission achieved, and think, "What next?" They are naturally motivated to look for the big picture. They more clearly set the direction. They anticipate the changes in the environment and the curves in the road ahead. All of these are functions of vision. A map has no value for showing you how to get somewhere without two critical pieces of information—where you are today and where you are going. As Cerner has grown, I have learned to differentiate the "super managers" from executives. The super managers are highly competent, intelligent managers who will amaze you with their abilities to get from point A to point B. They are recognized for their talents and are naturally given a large amount of responsibility in your organization due their ability to produce business results. The way you know they are not executives, however, is that they focus only on process. It is just about execution to them. I compare them to the gifted quarterback who can throw the ball 70 yards in practice, but when the game starts cannot read the defense and is at risk of being sacked for big losses. The super managers are talented, to be sure, but they cannot be relied upon to make the right moves when there are no coaches on the field.

Your career can advance a long way with excellent management skills. Cerner is in a much better position, however, if every manager is also an executive. If you develop yourself into an executive early in your career, prior to anyone giving you an executive title, you will have no boundaries in business. I am convinced that, in major areas of responsibility, we need executives, not super managers. As I pass the 25th year in my chief executive role at Cerner, our ability to differentiate between the super manager and the super executive will be very important, particularly when we have to choose our next CEO.

Manager vs. Entrepreneur

One time I jumped out of a perfectly good airplane. The chute opened—a good thing. I believe that there are some decisions in business that are so big, and the course is so uncharted in your mind, that you have to take a leap to make the decision. Starting Cerner and jumping out of a plane had the very same leaping feeling.

Entrepreneurs have an ability to take an extraordinary amount of risk and still maintain their sanity. They can bet it all and sleep soundly at night. They are mutants in this risk-bearing ability. I am convinced that for long-term success, however, the entrepreneur must be able to develop into the good manager and executive along the way.

The entrepreneur's risk-taking ability and tendency is typically at odds with management sensibilities and order, which creates tension within the well-managed organization. Risk-taking begets variance and uncertainty around outcomes (results). Managers are conditioned and rewarded to eliminate variance. I believe that, after 25 years, Cerner's culture continues to be predominantly entrepreneurial. How our skills as managers should ideally relate to our entrepreneurial instincts will need to be the topic for a future writing. I believe strongly that, for a company to grow and continuously innovate over a long period of time, the phenomenon of risk-taking must be part of its culture. It may be a paradox: How does a well-run company tolerate managers who constantly take extraordinary chances? We need an answer.

There, in a nutshell, are the differences between managers and leaders, executives, and entrepreneurs. Managers are the subject of this book. Being a manager is not an entitlement, nor is it a payoff for good work done in the past. It is a job, just like any other, with a serious set of expectations. As a manager, you will be held to a high standard because you are responsible for our associates and assets. This is not a job everyone wants. Even among those who _do_ want it, not everyone will succeed in management.

CHAPTER ONE

Are you right for management? Equally important, but a different thing entirely—is management right for you? These are some of the topics we'll explore in the remainder of this chapter.

Do You Have the Essential Personal Attributes of a Manager?

Many people think that the essential qualifications of a manager are lengthy experience and a deep skill set in a particular subject matter. They think of managers as individuals whose experience and skills in a domain have earned them the right to be in a position of responsibility over that domain. Without a doubt, knowledge is golden at Cerner, and many positions require it. The value of experience, however, must not eclipse the importance of unchangeable personal attributes. Experience is a function of past work, and skills can be taught and learned. By the time you get to Cerner, however, the essential personal attributes I discuss next are in place—and usually cannot be changed.

Trustworthiness Above All

Trust is one of the most valuable things you can earn from other human beings. Trust is a subjective feeling others have toward you, but over time there will be plenty of objective evidence to support its existence or absence. That evidence comes from your *decisions* and *behavior*. You cannot order someone to trust you. The only way you will be trusted in the long term is to always be trustworthy. Trustworthiness, because it is earned, is more clearly a pure leadership attribute than it is a management attribute. As a manager, however, you must take the responsibility of establishing trust seriously. Internally, your actions reflect on all managers. Externally, your actions reflect on all associates. To the associates who report to you and to the clients you meet, there is often no separate identity of an organization called Cerner. There is only you. Cerner is trustworthy only through your actions as a Cerner associate.

Nothing is more important to you as a leader and manager than your trustworthiness. People will not follow those whom they do not trust. You simply never break the trust of a client, associate, or business partner, regardless of the circumstance. It is very easy to break trust. Once trust is broken, it seldom is restored. When good people stop trusting you as a manager, you begin failing. Even though associates have to obey your direction in the short term, they will begin looking for a way to leave your team, perhaps even leaving Cerner to escape you. Make sure that you do not give good associates reasons to leave.

Being trustworthy requires several ingredients. If any ingredient is missing, trust is missing.

The first ingredient in trustworthiness is personal integrity. We each have an internal compass that guides our choices between right and wrong. Your internal compass is calibrated by your own value system. Your adherence to your value system is your personal integrity. As a manager, your integrity is constantly being evaluated. You must demonstrate that you have a compass with a steady, true north.

Being trustworthy requires a high standard of personal integrity. Your integrity can never be compromised. There are never degrees of the truth or trust. Tell the truth, even if it has negative consequences. Your standard for determining right and wrong must be high and consistent.

Over time, your personal integrity will be tested by large _and_ small decisions. Without notice, a major decision will tempt you to do something wrong, either because the pain of doing the right thing seems too high or the reward of doing the wrong thing seems too great. Daily, you will encounter smaller tests in commonplace activities such as time and expense reporting. The two are connected. If you cheat on the small stuff, you have defined yourself. That is why a false time report or expense report has always been grounds for termination at Cerner.

Commit to doing the right thing always. Get your values in place before you have to use them. Wrong actions could destroy the trust people have in our whole management team and destroy all that we have worked to accomplish. Also, be a guide for others. If you see others doing the wrong thing, stop them. We have a lot of young people at Cerner for whom this is their first career out of college. Help them make the right decisions.

The second ingredient in trustworthiness is adherence to an ethical code. In addition to showing your integrity as an individual, you must also demonstrate the ability to follow a set of rules defined for the larger group. Behavior must be consistent across Cerner. To a person, we must always be honest, ethical, and lawful to demonstrate our character as a company. One definition of ethics is a "set of principles of right conduct." Cerner's Code of Conduct is a representation of who we are collectively as a company. As a Cerner manager, you should read it, know it, and work by it, and you should enforce it within your team. Your behavior is your responsibility, and your team's behavior is also your responsibility. Do not drop the ball.

The third ingredient in trustworthiness is professional competency. Professional competency is the basis of predictability when dealing with others. It is beyond the scope of your personal integrity and ethics. In the long term, no one will follow you if you do not know what you are doing.

People are naturally forgiving of a mistake now and then, but a pattern of incompetence will break their trust. If you are *not competent* to regularly deliver what you have promised, even if you are honest and won't consciously do the wrong thing (integrity and ethics), you won't be trusted. Whether your failure to deliver is the result of a lack of responsible behavior or a lack of professional competency, the net effect in destroying trust—and ultimately your management career—is the same. Clients need to be able to count on you, and so do other associates, managers, and shareholders. Use real names when making decisions and commitments, not "clouds" like *someone, corporate,* or *K.C.* Everyone needs to understand who is accountable. Make your commitments carefully. They are your promise to make future events happen. After you make a commitment, do everything in your power to do what you said. Make the tough decisions. Say NO when it is beyond your power or capability to accomplish something. Clients and other managers will respect an answer of "we will not do that for the following reasons" far more than silence and elapsed time on requests they have made of you. Cerner has made a mistake if you are in a position of responsibility and you are not competent.

Integrity, ethics, and competency—together they form the *trustworthiness* that is the bedrock of your ability to manage successfully. Are you trustworthy? If not, *please* do not manage for Cerner. As a manager of people, projects, processes, and property, your trustworthiness will be tested on a much greater scale than the average associate's trustworthiness, and your ability to pass these tests will reflect on the entire company.

Following are a couple of personal stories to illustrate how quickly well-intended management decisions can be viewed as breaking the trust in important relationships.

———————— CHAPTER ONE ————————

In 1994, a Cerner sales team was selling to a major academic health center in the United States. I got an unexpected call from the CEO one afternoon. He was upset with us, and he wanted me to know about it. I had never met him. He called me to tell me that our sales team lied to him. I told him that this was very serious, that our word was the most important thing to me, and that I would be up to see him the next week. I took the involved team leaders with me, but they were not welcome by the CEO to attend the meeting. As it turned out, at the center of the issue was not a lack of integrity, but ignorance on our team's part. The client had been clear that their organization's needs were for both a hospital and a clinic. Our standard practice at the time, the team had issued a price quote based on number of beds. Our team simply had no initial concept of the amount of volume in a clinic (no beds!) or the additional work it would take to satisfy the client's needs in the clinic. When our team realized that the scope of the project would be much greater than what they had pictured, they changed the terms of their bid during contract negotiations. I went to the meeting alone. The rest of the team nervously waited in the cafeteria. The CEO vented. Then, I told the truth: my team members were all very honest, but inexperienced. They did not understand the scope of the work, and when they did, their response was to change the quote. I told him our original offer was good, even though we had underbid the work. He accepted it. They have been one of our most important clients over the last ten years. We subsequently changed how we priced our applications.

In the spring of 2003, Carly Fiorina, then the CEO of HP, came to visit me. We are a very important relationship partner to HP. They are important to Cerner. We had a good meeting. I asked her some very tough strategic questions, which she handled well. At the end of the meeting, this CEO of a multi-billion dollar company sheepishly asked me if we could talk about another point. She said that she was concerned with an order for some disk drives that Cerner had sent back to HP. She went on to explain that HP had competed with

EMC and IBM for an order for some additional drives in the Cerner data center. In her view, Cerner had issued an RFP, HP had won the business, and they shipped the drives. During shipment, EMC, realizing that they had lost the business, cut their price. Cerner management accepted the revised bid and told HP to come get their disk drives off of our shipping docks. Carly's point was that she did not believe that this was the way a partner treats another partner. There are always two sides to every story. I committed to check out the situation and promised that Cerner would do the right thing. Our management team shared a slightly different version of the story, but in my opinion, they were allowing minor points to distract them from making the right decision. Do not get confused in the details. Your job as a manager is to always do the right thing. We accepted the HP shipment.

Beyond trustworthiness, what are the other personal attributes that are essential to a Cerner manager? Here are others I consider must-haves:

Fire Within

"There is an enormous number of managers who have retired on the job."
- Peter Drucker

We all have a certain amount of energy that we direct toward our professional lives. The source of this energy is like a fire within. In most cases, the brighter the fire, the better for the management team. Life events and professional events can affect the intensity of the fire, sometimes temporarily, other times permanently. If your fire is out, then your management career is over. You can be the most intelligent, talented manager at Cerner, but if you no longer have any energy, your team will suffer with you in a management role. You should step aside and look for a different role where you can rekindle your fire. There are a number of capable associates behind you who have the energy to grow quickly into your position.

Fairness & Consistency

The essence of dealing with people is for decisions to be grounded in fairness. This is a broad subject, but the unwavering application of sound judgment is at its center. Do not play favorites. Nothing is more de-motivating for associates on your team than for others to receive the rewards and recognition when they are the ones doing the work. Remember the golden rule—treat people how you want to be treated. Treat each associate in your organization the way you would like to be treated by those in the senior management group. This technique should never be limited by gender, age, race, or cultural differences. The essential attribute of fairness transcends all differences. Managers who are found to mistreat associates will no longer manage at Cerner.

A corollary to fairness is consistency. I still recall a example from my introductory psychology course in college in which, during an experiment, one group of rats was shocked every five minutes, while another group was shocked only once per hour, but on random intervals. The second group became neurotic. The rats in the first group were just fine—they just got a little tense every four minutes and fifty-five seconds. Hopefully, the implications for management are clear.

Your associates can overlook many of your flaws if you manage them with fairness and consistency. An umpire who calls a small strike zone is fair if he calls it in the same location every time and *the same for both teams*.

Openness to Change

A physician sent me a small plaque in the early 1980s that I still have in my office today. It reads, *People Fear Change More Than They Do Disaster*. Our business environment constantly changes, and we must change along with it or die. Cerner managers must welcome change as an opportunity for growth and improvement, and they must be ready to help others deal with it.

Change comes in many forms. Cerner enters new, unfamiliar markets and domains. We get larger, obsoleting our organizational structures. Our healthcare environment changes as a result of new medical capabilities and knowledge. Information technology rapidly changes, obsoleting layers in our architecture. Notably, change is the goal behind everything we do as a company. We come to work every day with the assumption that we must change the healthcare system to eliminate all avoidable error, inappropriate variance, unnecessary waste, needless delay, and costly friction.

The only constant is change. As a manager, you must manage to change yourself along with your responsibilities and environment. You must drive extraordinary change from within while remaining sensitive to associates' and clients' fears. Growth creates change, and change creates growth.

Edge

All managers make decisions. Good managers have the edge to make swift, principled, difficult decisions. You cannot be a successful manager if you *avoid* conflict and risk. Many management decisions are rife with conflict and risk. Saying no to a client's request when it doesn't fit our priorities, "walking" the bad business deal at the end of a tough quarter, firing a nonperforming associate who is also a friend—all of these take edge. Making the decision in 1994 to build *HNA Millennium* took edge. It was risky, but it was the right thing to do. Edge involves risk and timing, and it also involves right and wrong. Firing people indiscriminately is not edge. Being inappropriately harsh is not edge.

Many managers have a hard time making tough decisions regarding people, so they drag their feet or don't do anything. Avoiding, passing, or deferring a tough personnel issue is the mark of a poor manager. When the situation calls for it, a good manager must be able to give immediate, tough feedback, deliver a negative review, put someone on a performance plan, or fire someone. At times you may be able to coach a better performance out of a person or find a better fit for them within the company, but not always. In my opinion one of the very worst things you can do as a manager is to transfer an associate with a performance problem to another team rather than having the edge to deal with the situation personally. One impact is that the associate continues to operate under the delusion that nothing is wrong with his or her performance, depriving the associate of the chance to become a more valuable contributor. A more devastating impact is that it will now take the next manager many months to make a fair determination as to the associate's performance, costing both the hiring manager and company the consequences of having a poor-performing associate *and* the opportunity to have replaced that associate with a qualified, motivated associate. You wouldn't like it if someone did this to you, so don't do it to someone else. It weakens the team.

Another dimension of edge is casting aside the *need* to be liked. I think that having a strong need to be liked is the biggest reason why otherwise good, smart, motivated associates should not become managers. It is a very natural tendency to want to be liked. It starts early in life on the playground, where your popularity is a measure of success, and it continues throughout life. Many people never learn how to set this tendency aside for the sake of sound judgment. They let their need to be liked interfere with their ability to do the right thing at the right time, because they simply do not want to upset people.

The old verbiage was that it is "lonely at the top"—you were never to become friends with the people whom you manage. There is wisdom in that admonition, but it is difficult to implement. You experience a great number of exciting events with your team. You go into battle, with exhilarating victories and painful defeats. They are bright, personable people. Of course you will develop some of your best friendships in life inside the workplace, and the reporting relationship will be quite invisible in your interactions with one another. How I have dealt with this over the years has been to be very clear with everyone: I will always make my decisions in my role based on what is best for Cerner—not you, not Neal, and not anyone else—just Cerner.

Develop a sharp edge in your management habits. Teach yourself to address on a timely basis the big, tough decisions that must be made. Please do not take the easy route; it will harm your team, your career, and Cerner.

Loyalty to the Enterprise

It is hard to be on a team you do not believe in; as a manager, you are also expected to know and support the direction of Cerner with your team. This does not mean that you have to agree with 100 percent of the decisions that are made within Cerner. Respectful arguing and even strong disagreement are a healthy part of team life and improve our decisions. I will many times choose to argue the minority view simply to test the thinking of the majority. Modeling how to argue in a constructive way is part of your job as a manager. What is not healthy is for you to lead your team in opposing Cerner's decisions, direction, or leaders. Once a decision has been made, it is your role as a manager to carry it out. Although you might not agree with every decision, you should know and share the context of all big decisions with your team. Give them the *why* behind the decision.

I have seen too many cases in which the manager exposes *major and sustained* differences with the company's direction to his or her team. It is very unwise, and the manager should be terminated. Disagree, please! But disagree privately and directly with the ones who have made the decisions you think are wrong. This is not a democracy. You are not campaigning for votes. Quick and cheap popularity points have little long-term value, and your team's perception of you as an authority will be undermined if they see that you are in opposition to Cerner and its leaders. An organization or team that operates under the leadership of a critical manager who has lost faith in Cerner tends to take on a "doomed" feeling, and the associates on such a team are robbed of the ability to share in Cerner's victories. If you, as a manager, find that you fundamentally and irrevocably disagree with Cerner's direction, then managing for Cerner no longer makes sense. You will do everyone, including yourself, a service by finding a new place where your energy is not wasted.

A frequent, related mistake made by many managers is to hide behind the proverbial *they* pronoun. *They* say we have to work this weekend; *they* say we have to have our time reports in on Friday. I was in the Army National Guard. It was in basic training that *they* first caught my attention. The drill sergeant never wanted us to think that he had anything to do with the fact that we were going to march/run 15 miles to the rifle range in the heat of the day or that we were not going to get leave on the weekend. It was always *they* who ordered him do it to us. I became fascinated with who *they* were. Well, a few years later when we started Cerner, I had a flashback to my military service—I must be *they*. I am here to tell you—as *they*—that there is a reason for everything we (*they*) do. Your job as a manager is to understand that reason and convey that *why* message rather than the *they* message. If you are using the pronoun *they*, you are failing as a manager. If your team is using *they*, **you** are failing.

Do You Have the Personality & Style To Be an Effective Manager?

There is a slight difference between personality and style. Personality is more basic and has to do with a person's intrinsic temperament, character, and mentality. While sometimes related to personality, style is an outward expression, a characteristic way of acting, expressing, or performing.

There are many personality types that can be successful as managers, some on seemingly opposite ends of the spectrum. It is actually easier to describe what *doesn't* work than what does. In my experience, some types of personalities shy away from the front-line, high-pressure nature of management. Most associates prefer to be in off-stage roles and do not want to be on the spot, accountable as the person in charge of the team. They are happy to remain individual contributors. Some are very cautious by nature and do not have any taste for taking risks or being in conflict with others. For those who naturally shy away, it is best not to press the issue. You should not encourage a career path for yourself or others that fights nature. Cerner needs many backstage associates. It's not a character fault if that is what the associate wants.

Some personalities do not work for outright negative reasons. Some managers cannot detach themselves from their own large egos in order to fairly represent the interests of their own teams. Some do not have a value system that respects other people and clients. Others are not certain enough of their own skills to make real management decisions.

One of my least favorite personalities is that of the perpetual victim. Trust me, in this world, there are some real victims. But perpetual victims *always* point to external reasons as their excuse for why something failed to happen. You will find that these are the same people who say *they* a lot. Victims make very poor managers. Our job as managers is to produce results, not excuses! I hate excuses, and I try to avoid people who portray themselves as victims.

Similar to personalities, I also believe there are a very large number of *styles* that are effective in management. Again, it is easier to discuss the ones that do not fit. There are five management styles that can be effective elsewhere in the world, but have NO PLACE at Cerner:

The first I would call *Command and Control*, a very military model in which people are ordered to follow with no chance for input into the decision. I will explain why this style does not work later in the book.

The second is the *Abusive* manager who uses his or her power as manager to mistreat associates working for him or her. Interestingly, often this manager's manager may never see this behavior, because the abuser acts very differently in relationships *up* the chain of command—sometimes earning this style the designation *Kiss Up, Kick Down*.

The third is the *Micromanager*. We simply have too much to do and have too many smart associates for our managers to waste critical time giving detailed instructions. We must trust our teams.

The fourth is the *Empire Builder*, whose motives are focused on amassing power and advancing his or her personal career. This manager is naturally incented to build and protect a strong team in pursuit of his or her goals, but cannot be trusted to make decisions that are in the best interest of the company and its other managers.

The fifth is the *Insecure Manager* who takes personal credit for the team's successes and quickly passes the blame for any failures of the team to the team members. This manager robs the emotional energy of the team and hides from the rest of the organization the talent inside his or her team. This manager utterly fails to understand the manager's obligation to *Manage i*T with a small *i* and a big Team.

Do You Want To Be a Manager? —Let's Think

Up to this point, we've discussed whether you are right for management. Now, I want to turn your attention to a different matter entirely— whether management is right for you.

Some of my favorite questions to pose to young associates are "What do you want to be when you grow up? What do you want to be doing five years from now?" It is quite natural for many associates to want to be in big management positions. I love it when they say that they want my job as CEO. That indicates that they have a really big fire within.

My answer to the question: "I do not want to grow up!"

In all seriousness, however, please consider the topics in the following sections when evaluating whether you really want to be a manager.

Dr. Peter's Advice

Most everyone has heard of *The Peter Principle*. This was described in a short book by the same title written by Dr. Laurence J. Peter. It basically says that *in a hierarchically structured organization, people tend to be promoted up to their "level of incompetence"*. His philosophy has two premises at its core. His first concept is that almost all organizations will promote the person who exceeds in performing in lower ranks until they are in management. The second concept is that, through continuing to climb the organization's hierarchical ladder, even a competent person will eventually reach a level in that organization at which he or she will be inadequate and will begin to fail. Dr. Peter also surmises that organizations have trouble "demoting" individuals, thus their ranks become clogged with inadequate management. His theory seems sound to me.

A corollary to Dr. Peter's promotion theory is a phenomenon that happens in high-growth companies. As the organization grows, a person who remains in the same position, with the very same title and job, finds that the demands of that role grow significantly. The "same" management role in a 50, 500, and 5,000-person organization is radically different. I am fully aware how the Peter Principle can easily apply to me as CEO.

Implicit in Dr. Peter's principle is that many people enjoy the rewards of being an individual contributor on the team, not being responsible for the team. No matter how you get there, it is no fun being in a management position at which you will not excel. What happens if you find yourself in the wrong position? It does happen. If you do nothing, then typically, over time, you develop a performance problem that grows so large it becomes visible inside the organization. Someone in management, usually without context, makes a decision to replace you. Your evaluation is changed down, and your future with Cerner is in jeopardy.

What should you do if you are promoted against your better judgment, or if you find that your abilities in your role no longer fit the growing company? Tell your manager. Tell your manager's manager. Tell them that you do not like having the responsibility for others and that your personal mission and passion is for doing quality work inside the organization, but not managing. We need experts at Cerner that are very good at what they do, and do it each and every day. There is nothing wrong with not wanting to manage people. Tell them that the job has grown beyond your ability to do it well and that you want to find a place in the organization where you are better equipped to contribute. Whatever the truth is, tell it to them.

Do You Want a Large "Family"?

In my experience, many associates want to be in charge of people, and the more the merrier. There is always a bit of naiveté, however, in their desires. Dealing with people will be the most challenging aspect of managing. Few realize how the responsibility, accountability, and workload of managing others will change their professional lives. Few understand in advance that their career satisfaction will forevermore be based on the team's accomplishments, not on their individual contribution. I have always compared the difference between being a manager and a non-manager to the difference between being a parent and a college student. It is a completely new paradigm, and the freedom you experienced before the family is now gone. Your actions are setting the example for each family member. As a manager, you have the responsibility to help each individual manage his or her own career and professional issues. This is a huge responsibility, and you need to take it very seriously. Your role is to nurture and develop your associates, to qualify them for additional responsibilities, and to give them wings (promote them) when they are ready. No longer do you have that carefree feeling of being accountable for only yourself. Evaluate carefully whether this sounds rewarding to you.

Your Aptitudes & Inclinations

Sometimes individuals' aptitudes will direct and shape their career paths away from management roles. Many people are skilled at organizing, executing, creating, and delivering, but they are not motivated by being in charge (as long as they trust their managers and leaders). They simply want to be the best at their chosen profession. Much of Cerner's valuable Intellectual Property is *created* by extremely gifted people who have little or no desire to manage and want to create through designing and developing sophisticated solutions to complex problems in healthcare. This is their art. Likewise, across the company, there are sales associates, consultants, instructors, writers, testers, builders, troubleshooters, and "firefighters" who create immense value for Cerner by pursuing excellence in their given domain. That is why we created two distinct career tracks years ago: Management and Domain. Opportunities for career development, rewards, and advancement exist in both tracks. You should never feel that becoming a manager is the only way to advance your career.

Your Circumstances

There are times when an associate's circumstances will dictate his or her role. I am not a believer in part-time management. Management by its nature—that is, responsibility for others—is a full-time commitment.

Even full-time associates can have outside interests, life circumstances, or rigorous obligations that are at odds with a management career. In your life, you are entitled to choose the exact priorities that make sense for you. Management is not compatible with every choice. Evaluate your circumstances and priorities honestly.

If you want to be the CEO, but you are unwilling to travel, your likelihood of success is minimal. Sometimes an associate accepts the manager role, but is unwilling to make the adjustments in behavior and lifestyle needed to be an effective manager. It causes all kinds of conflict for the new manager, and the team is not well led. It is important to consciously understand the responsibilities and role that you have agreed to as a manager.

A Final Consideration on Work-Life Balance—A Huge Challenge

In a high-growth, high-intensity, high-purpose company, it can be very difficult to balance the work demands with the life demands. In management, the work demands are sometimes higher than they would be in a non-management role. There are no formulas for achieving equilibrium, and every individual has a unique set of values that drives a personal equation. I believe that balance is required. I personally call my attempt at balance HAL—Have A Life.

I developed a strong point of view in the early years, when the demands were extreme on just about every associate at Cerner. (I know that extreme demands still live on at Cerner, but I am specifically referring to the kind of primitive pressure that comes from needing to survive by killing today what you will eat tonight.) Although the pressures have morphed somewhat, I still like my basic supposition that, for the highly motivated associate, Cerner must be in the top three life priorities, with the sequence being an individual choice. While everyone's list can be different, the most common three life priorities are family, faith, and firm. When softball or day trading becomes a higher priority than Cerner, that associate should not be included in our management team.

A long time ago, I saved a saying, attributed to an old English prayer, that I thought expresses the idea of a well-balanced life:

> *Take time to work, it is the price of success.*
>
> *Take time to think, it is the source of power.*
>
> *Take time to play, it is the secret of perpetual youth.*
>
> *Take time to read, it is the foundation of wisdom.*
>
> *Take time to dream, it is hitching your wagon to a star.*
>
> *Take time to love and be loved, it is the privilege of the gods.*
>
> *Take time to look around, it is too short a day to be selfish.*
>
> *Take time to laugh, it is the music of the soul.*

I never pass up an opportunity to watch a sunset. For me, it is a great daily reminder of how precious and fleeting life is.

NEAL PATTERSON

****

If you look at the questions raised in this chapter, you will likely find that they are easy to answer...you either *do* or *don't* have all the necessary attributes and desire to be a Cerner manager. If after reading this you're still convinced that you are right for management *and* it is right for you, read on!

Chapter Two

Managing To Be a Manager

Your environment...is the perfect reflection of your habitual thinking.
Thought rules the world.
– Joseph Edward Murphy

It must be in the water, but most inexperienced, first-time managers believe that there is some magic potion, book, or course they must drink, read, or take before they know what to do. I wish. This is *a* book; it's not THE book. Yes, there will likely be *a* course to take, but it won't be THE course.

Once you are promoted to management, you will start to become involved in setting corporate vision and strategy—just like in the popular management books. But the biggest change after the promotion is the amount of e-mail you will receive, the number of meetings you will go to, and the influx of administrative and planning duties you must do for your team members.

It is likely that you know how to do the work. If you are new to the organization or area, get to know your team and clients well. From day one, you will have inherited some commitments and probably a set of significant operational problems as well.

Get calm. Get the big picture. Get organized. Get a plan. Get to work. Quit worrying, and quit thinking someone else is going to tell you how to do this. Just think about it, use your common sense, intelligence, skills, and talents—the strongest potion you will find.

I'm not saying that you have nothing to learn about being a manager. In fact, your need to learn has just increased a lot. Trial and error will be your greatest teacher. The least painful path is to learn from the trials and errors of *others*. Reading is one way to do this. Some of the management truths I rely on daily have been gleaned from other people's stories. Observing is another technique for learning from others. Very early in my career, I learned to study the attributes, habits, and techniques of highly successful executives. It was probably the greatest single aid in my development. A genuine mentoring relationship with a manager you admire is great if you can get it. If you can't, however, you can still model yourself—and your career—after someone else from afar.

In the previous chapter, I talked about personal attributes, personalities, preferences, and needs that are essentially unchangeable. If you have ever been back to one of your high school reunions, you will probably agree that the vast majority of people do not change much as they age. Nature and early nurturing impact us a lot, and our core personality and intelligence are not easily altered. But we are also creatures of habit, and when motivated sufficiently, we can change our habits.

In this chapter, I would like to discuss habits and techniques that you can, with discipline, learn. *Warning: This chapter is quite pedestrian.* In later chapters, I will discuss more complex topics such as vision and developing business strategy. Here I am dealing with what you do when you get out of bed. And again, I am not trying to be prescriptive, just communicating what has worked for me over my career.

Time Management: Plan *i*T

Time is your first management challenge. It is the most perishable resource we manage. It simply vanishes. We either use it or lose it—our choice. Personal time management is an essential habit that you *must* develop. Only you can control your use of time. As a manager, your environment places huge demands on your time. *It will control you* and render you ineffective as a manager if you do not manage it.

When you become a manager, your schedule instantly starts to become more crowded. I consider my schedule to be a large part of my "windshield." The other big windshield items for me are e-mail and phone—I turned off phone mail. The "windshield effect" is the demand for my time and attention that is determined by things that appear in the present. The faster you drive, the more things hit your windshield. While there are many great topics appearing on my schedule, they are by nature usually determined by others—clients, defined business processes, other associates, business partners, HAL (Have A Life), and still others. Most of these types of windshield items are not designed to produce the business results that you are responsible to deliver. Typically, they are about some other manager's responsibilities, or they are things that are important to other associates who need you to take action on them. Many new managers make the mistake of being victimized by their calendars. If you are going to be highly effective, you must carefully control the utilization of your time. You must be able to answer these questions: Who is in charge of my time? Am I working on the right thing today, this hour? (Answer key: "You" and "Yes".)

Proactive time management involves making a *plan* for how to spend your time. In this section, I will describe some of the habits I've developed. *Note:* Plan *in this section refers to personal time and effort planning, not the business plans you will create for your area of responsibility as a manager. There is a strong relationship between the two, however.* My system of time management consists of daily, weekly, and annual routines. Each routine is integrated with the others. The weekly routine is the one in which I create the core plan for how I will spend my time and drive my goals in the short term (next two weeks) and intermediate term (next 100 days). It really is where I discern my priorities. Both the daily and weekly routines guard my time against the damage that would otherwise be caused by my environment and the windshield effect.

Personal Daily Plan

I try very hard to get ready for each day with at least one hour of advance preparation, reflection, and contemplation of the day's events. Unfortunately, morning is my preferred time of day for such reflection. In the evening, my mind is fragmented by the day's events, and my battery is low. Plus, if I load my mind up with tomorrow's events, my brain is working on them all night, and I almost always wake up at 2:30 A.M. This first priority of the day is so important to me, that if I have a 6:30 A.M. flight, I usually get up at 4:00 A.M. (the unfortunate part) to have an hour of quiet time. Your optimal planning time may differ from mine. Regardless, do take some time to plan each day. You will more than recoup your planning time in effectiveness.

Personal Weekly Plan

I start every week with a defined routine, with one to three hours either Sunday evening or Monday morning. I carefully review each scheduled event for the next two weeks, creating a hand-written, two-week schedule in my journal. You may think this schedule is redundant with my Outlook calendar, but it is not. Rewriting my schedule gives me the time to re-think how well the schedule is using my time. I scan the upcoming 100 days on my calendar but do not make a copy of this. In parallel with this calendar review, I systematically create a "matrix checklist" in five categories (rows) with two dimensions of time each (columns), for a total of 10 boxes (see diagram). The names of the five categories illustrate my propensity to focus on *action verbs* that succinctly describe the "what" that requires my attention. The two dimensions of time represent immediate things, and things that are not immediate. I borrowed the columns from Stephen Covey's "Urgent" and "Not Urgent".

Weekly Planner

Categories	Immediate	Not Immediate
■ **Prepare** *(Events I must prepare for)*		
■ **Act** *(Things I must do)*		
■ **Decide** *(Decisions I must make)*		
■ **Achieve** *(Results I must achieve)*		
■ **Think** *(Mental frameworks I must create)*		

Figure 2.1 – Weekly Planner

If you want to try this, the Immediate column is your windshield, the things you must do, important to the present, the execution of yesterday's plan. Most people are controlled by the present. I have tried to develop a strong instinct and discipline to get major work done on the Not

Immediate tasks. Your ability to create the future is a function of how much time you work in the Not Immediate area. The most important row in this table is Decide. It is here that I make sure to capture the tough (requiring edge) decisions that must be made. The fifth row called Think helps me focus on upcoming decisions, creating the mental framework for understanding the evolution of our business.

I am still amazed about how valuable this private weekly think time is for achieving major business results. The very few times I miss starting a week with this routine, I am anxious all week long about whether I am spending my time wisely.

The Quarterly Plan and Report

In our world as a public company, a quarter has a lot of significance. A 90-day cycle is an adequate amount of time in which to drive significant achievements.

I have always liked the idea of requiring all of us as *managers* to document and publish to our own managers our goals and objectives for the upcoming quarter, along with how our actual results compared against the preceding quarter's forecast. I have never insisted, however, that this be a mandatory practice. We have a handful of quarterly processes in which our significant business functions are required to prepare forecasts for the next quarter along with a rolling four-quarter view. The most visible of these management practices is our Quarterly Business Review, which gives a detailed view of the sales, consulting, and operational areas of our business. It is an indispensable method for running our business. Every quarter, we are also held accountable for some of the previous quarter's results by way of SEC filings and our reports to Wall Street.

It makes sense that the quarterly approach to forecasting and reviewing should be extended to each manager. It could be that the natural quarterly business cycle and processes consume too much of our available time to do this. Personally, I take the time each quarter to write a memo to the members of Cerner's Board of Directors. In it, I analyze the current results relative to our plans, discuss the changes in our business environment, and define the expected future results. You should consider having each associate who works directly for you write a quarterly report. If you are a manager with major client responsibilities, you should send a similar report to the client's senior executive management, highlighting Cerner's accomplishments during the past 90 to 180 days and what is expected during the next period—it is a good practice.

Personal Annual Plan

I love using a year to measure progress in both my professional and my personal life. I find one year to be enough time to measure real progress against my goals and objectives.

The method that I have used for a number of years is to spend some time writing during the period between Christmas and New Year. I first develop an annual schedule by reviewing the upcoming year's schedule and posting the major events on my "Year at a Glance" spreadsheet. It is scary to see how many specific days of the year are already committed before you start the year. At the beginning of 2005, I have 229 days either pre-committed or expected of me, and that is before any personal time. Here are some of my commitments:

- *Client Events – Cerner-sponsored executive forums and annual Cerner Health Conference; HIMSS conference; multiple investment* community meetings; plus a list of alphabet-soup industry meetings, each usually meeting two to three times per year, at which my attendance as Cerner's CEO ranges from desired to expected. I won't spell out the names, but you can look them up if you are curious: HRDI, HMA CEO, HMA CMO, CCI, and HEN.

• Internal Cerner – Board of Director meetings, quarterly processes, Executive Cabinet meetings, CinC Associate Conferences, business reviews of key milestones, Think Weeks, executive reviews.

• Client CEO to CEO – Pre-committed engagement reviews, targeted client connections, road shows in which I spend a full week traveling and connecting with CEOs of major health systems.

• Healthcare Policy – Trips to Washington, D.C., Board of Advisors meetings with RAND, meetings with states and state organizations.

• Wall Street – I am down to two or three investor conferences at which I am expected to present, plus the quarterly conference calls and any firefighting.

• Business to Business – Meetings with other CEOs interested in relationships with Cerner and vice versa.

• Community Commitments – I am extremely careful with non-Cerner commitments—a caution that I encourage in others. But every manager should have some community involvement. I have two things to which I commit personal time and energy through a variety of vehicles. One is improving the entrepreneurial

*environment in the Kansas City region, and the other is keeping our
modern society in touch with its agricultural roots. Both require a major
time commitment.*

- *Friends, Family, Fun, and HAL – Significant holidays, routine
  family and friend events, spring break with the kids, a couple of
  quick hunting trips, a good fishing trip every other year, and family
  vacation. I also try to satisfy my desire for adventure in this
  category. In 2004, I completed the last leg of a Lewis and Clark
  journey with my youngest son, Will, and my best friend from
  college, following (in a car) the Lewis and Clark Trail from Kansas
  City to the Pacific Ocean. It took three weeks of travel broken into
  three different legs over a five-year period of time to accomplish this.*

After developing an annual schedule, I turn my attention to two
separate but related electronic documents, one professional and the other
personal. I treat both as private journals in which I write my completely
honest reflections and assessments of the events, accomplishments, and
struggles of past year. I state my major goals and objectives for the next
year and beyond, and I also spend time thinking and writing about the
key relationships in my professional and personal life. Both of these have
become sizeable documents, between 30 to 50 pages, and I simply update
them from year to year. I would estimate that I spend 30 to 40 hours
working on the combination of the two each year. This exercise requires
a fair amount of reflection on both the past and the future. It has been
during this time that I have realized some of my biggest insights, the true
Aha! moments, and have made some weighty decisions about Cerner.
The time is worth it. I strongly recommend you develop a similar habit.

Get Organized: Journal *i*T, Note *i*T, File *i*T

I am a gadget guy by nature. I am somewhat obsessed with the digitization of our culture. I am usually an early adopter of personal organization and communication technologies. I was carrying computers onto airplanes as soon as the first *luggables* were announced. (Most of you do not know what a luggable is—it was a computer that was the maximum allowable size of carry-on luggage and weighed more than 30 pounds.)

As eager as I am to hasten the completely digital age, I still use physical, paper journals to document the actual events in my days. It could be my compulsive nature, but to me it is very important to carefully number each journal and document its from/to date range. I document my weekly plan, described earlier, inside this journal. If you have ever seen me in a meeting, perhaps you have noticed my habit of creating an entry for each meeting, always documenting the subject, day of week, date, and those present. It is amazing how many times, sometimes years later, I will access the journal to look for information about a meeting or find the picture I drew during the meeting. I have never mastered how to record unscheduled phone calls. I do try to take notes in my journal on important topics that arise during phone calls.

With every meeting, you always walk out with a load of paper, which I usually keep. I file this in a color-coded week file. As I plan and start every week, I create a purple folder with the week number. By this, I mean the sequential week number of the year, for example, Week #31-2004. (It helps if you select the "Show Week Numbers" option in Calendar Options in Microsoft Outlook.) I file all loose paper documents in the week file. I stack the week files at my home office during the year. And at the end of the year, I put them away. Laugh if you want, but give me a meeting over the last 15 years, and I am able to produce the documents that were used in the meeting. The access method does require some recollection of the existence of the meeting. If it is searchable in Outlook, then it is easy. If not, I guess the time frame and review each weekly plan for the event.

The digital world requires its own strategy, particularly if you have multiple devices to keep in sync. I have found that it is easier to process a large volume of e-mail if I use rules to pre-sort it into separate inboxes by distribution list. I separate the mail in which I am carbon copied (Cc) from the messages in which I am the direct addressee. I confess, if there is a large distribution on an e-mail message, I do not read it. If a great number of Cerner managers are aware of something, I work on the supposition that I cannot add further value. I have a defined set of directories where I file the e-mail, Word documents, Excel spreadsheets, PowerPoint presentations, and network files. The search engines (particularly Google Desktop Search) are great, but logical organization is still very important.

While I am advocating meticulous note-keeping, I should point out that there is another school of thought in which no documentation is preferred. This is because your e-mail messages, journals, notes, and files are discoverable as evidence in legal proceedings. I have been on the witness stand being cross-examined by a plaintiff's attorney while looking at a poster-sized version of my well-organized weekly plan from my journal. We won the case. Do the right thing for the right reason every day. Do not live in fear.

Organizational strategies and systems vary widely. Here, my intent is not to force my organizational system on you, but to give you the sense that it's important to be accountable for *information* in the same way that you would be for material property, were it in your charge. The key is to have a highly reliable, repeatable, predefined personal system that is ingrained into your daily habits.

NEAL PATTERSON

THINK Using Problem-Solving Tools & Techniques

Academics talk about critical thinking skills. The entrepreneur and founder of IBM, Thomas J. Watson, made it his company motto: THINK. I can almost hear his emphatic pleas to the IBM management to...THINK. *Think* is an amazing verb. It works. It is the source of solutions to problems, the creation of new ideas. It is the fountain .: which you will make thousands and thousands of business decisions in your career as a manager. The alternative to think is react. Please think.

Over the years, I seem to repeatedly use a small set of methods to approach thinking about business problems and opportunities. They are basic models that invite new dimensions of thinking. Once again, there is no science here, just things that work for me.

Draw the Big Picture

You may have heard the old adage, "If you can't get it on one page, then you don't understand it." Although my guess is that this statement was first made about someone writing a memo, I think it's also a great rule of thumb for anyone attempting to graphically represent a plan. I am a big believer in the value of drawing a single-page picture of a concept or plan. A drawing forces more understanding of the relationships of the variables than a simple list would. You can create more context in a picture. Your artistic skill is secondary. Learn to draw.

Over the years, Cliff (very artistic), Jeff Townsend (another senior executive who is also an artistic abstract thinker), and I (not so artistic) have gotten proficient at drawing a picture of the output from any given Think Week or SWOT session. These are techniques that will be described later in this chapter. The pictures we draw serve as a single icon of our group thinking and are sometimes quite complex.

A one-page picture does not need to be understood by every outsider who views it. Its complexity may be a little mystifying to those who did not participate in creating it. That is not to say that others will not obtain some ancillary benefit from it. The way the various iterations of Cerner's Community Health Model image have been used to educate associates, clients, and shareholders is a great example of how others profit from a well-executed single-page picture.

You can see the complexity but also detect the crystallization of some important ideas in the Big Picture outputs from three different Think Week strategy sessions we conducted: Tan-Tar-A in 1994 (Figure 2.2). Big Cedar in 1999 (Figure 2.3), and Flint Oaks in 2002 (Figure 2.4). If you squint hard enough, you may be able to see the actual progression of the Cerner vision over the span of years represented in these pictures.

The Tan-Tar-A Strategy

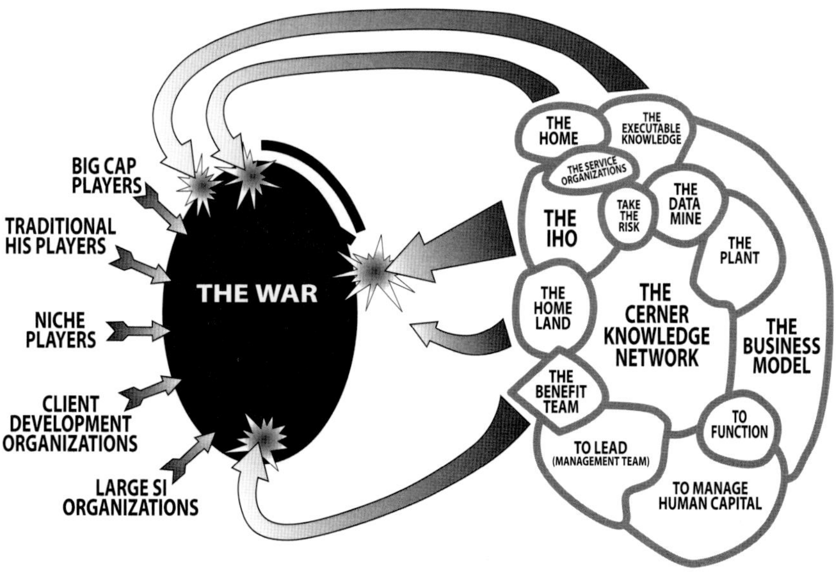

Figure 2.2 – Big Picture, circa 1994, Tan-Tar-A Think Week

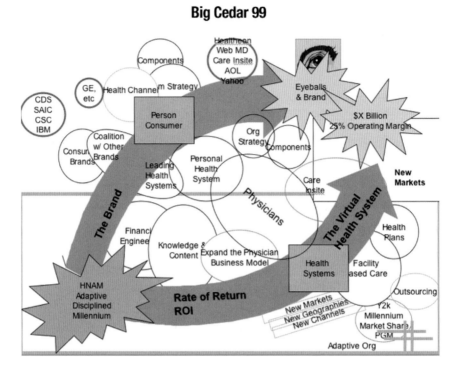

Figure 2.3 – Big Picture, circa 1999, Big Cedar Think Week

SWOT Analysis

The SWOT analysis is a must in your managerial toolkit. We have used it effectively through the entire history of Cerner. It is a simple framework for focusing on your organization's Strengths, Weakness, Opportunities, and Threats (SWOT). It also can be used to analyze a competitor. Although you can perform this exercise by yourself, it works best with a skilled facilitator leading a group to brainstorm each of these variables for the organization.

To perform a SWOT analysis, start by challenging the group to think about two distinct contexts, Environmental and Internal, for the issue, unit, or enterprise you are analyzing.

Big Picture, Flint Oaks Think Week

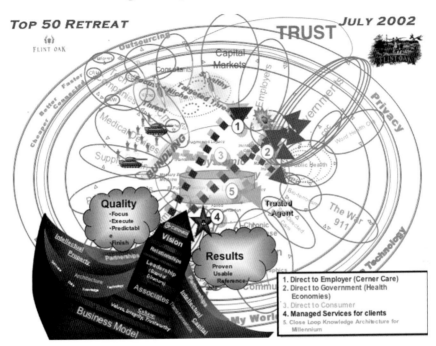

Figure 2.4 – Big Picture, circa 2002, Flint Oaks Think Week

Next, use your combined thinking power to generate the SWOT variables. I prefer to start with the Environment, listing and describing both the Threats and Opportunities that exist in your External environment and that you have little or no control over. The environmental factors are a given. Your business plans must address these. Next, examine and brainstorm the Strengths and Weaknesses for your Internal context. Because they are internal, you have control over these as a management team. Again, list and describe these.

The art involved in this exercise is to find the relationships between the SWOT variables. You will immediately find that every Threat creates an Opportunity, and every Strength becomes a Weakness. The SWOT variables will tend to form clusters.

Define and label the clusters. Build a plan to address each cluster. Using the technique from the previous section, draw the Big Picture that represents your SWOT analysis of the environments, the clusters, and your plan to address them. It is likely that the picture will be busy looking.

Here is the output of the Environment we created from a July 2002 SWOT analysis. If you look closely, you will see that it was the basis for the Flint Oaks Big Picture on the previous page.

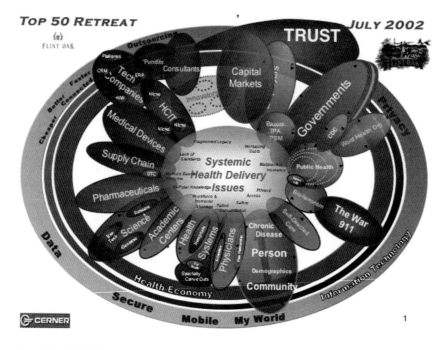

Figure 2.5 – SWOT Environment, circa 2002, Flint Oaks

Doing SWOT analysis in a small group is both fun and insightful. The optimal number of participants is between 6 and 15, though I have done it with as many as 50. Everyone in the group will be surprised with the output and very pleased to have been directly involved in setting direction and strategy.

Four-Box Analysis

The four-box analysis is a simple, quick, and extremely powerful technique that can be applied to many business problems. I use it to quickly visualize the relationship of two important variables when developing business strategies. I do not recommend using the four-box as a discovery technique for new ideas. Instead, it is a powerful focusing technique to create clarity around a major decision and to test your understanding of the consequences of your decision.

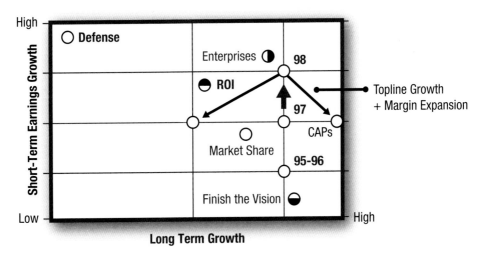

Figure 2.6 – Four-Box Analysis, circa 1998, Cerner's Strategy Choices

Figure 2.6 on the preceding page depicts a four-box model developed at a 1998 planning session. It shows the tradeoffs involved in some of Cerner's strategy choices. The strategies, as well as a couple of structure choices, were plotted according to their effects on two variables: the often conflicting goals of short-term bottom line growth and long-term top line growth. Some of the dots with dates indicate prior period strategies and structures, revealing how, over time, we shifted Cerner's focus from the long-term growth strategy of broad vision, as we began _HNA Millennium_, to strategies such as individual enterprises that created _both_ long-term growth benefits and short-term return to the shareholders through increased operating margins. As a manager, you constantly deal with seemingly contradictory options, and you usually have to balance the choices. Often a given period of time dictates a bias toward one choice, and over time you sway back toward the other. Never assume you are on the right path. Constantly rethink your options.

As a manager, you are responsible for keeping your organization healthy. At the enterprise level, that means growing it. At the same 1998 meeting, we used another four-box diagram (Figure 2.7 on the facing page) to parse the relationship between different markets and solutions. Each cell of the four-box creates a clear picture of the management requirements necessary to develop and implement strategies to grow our business in the parameters defined by that cell. Growing your business with existing solutions inside existing markets (hospitals) is quite different from creating new solutions and selling to new markets.

To do a four-box analysis, draw a box, and then draw a vertical and horizontal hatch, creating four boxes or quadrants. On the X-axis write the most important attribute of the decision or strategic direction you are considering. On the Y-axis write the second most important attribute of

Cerner's 1998-2000 Growth Strategies

New

	Existing
1. Invest in NHO 2. Invest in HS sales leader 3. Invest in sales leader for HNV, Capstone 4. Start MC enterprise? **2, 500%** **I**	1. Invest in NHO at process level, enterprises 2. Build country level sales engine **3, 500%** **II**
1. Develop relationship strategy 2. Develop CS account growth strategy 3. P.S. Benefits sales strategies, services **1, 100%** **IV**	1. Shift resources from regions to enter. 2. Hire incremental resources, enter. 3. Develop CAP strategy for existing clients **4, 20%** **III**

Markets (left axis) Existing (bottom left)

Solutions & Services

Figure 2.7 – Four-Box Analysis, circa 1998, Cerner's 1998-2000 Growth Strategies

the decision or direction. Then on each axis, create a relevant bipolar scale (*bipolar* in the sense of being able to express a continuum between two opposite or contradictory ideas, such as high-to-low, expensive-to-cheap, or large-to-small). Then brainstorm the decision or idea to see what responses belong in each of the four quadrants.

Do several four-boxes on each decision, changing the X-Y attributes. Presto, you will be shocked with the clarity gained in a very short time. You have to build a framework to look at your decision, strategic choice, or idea.

Fishbone

I am a visual thinker. Along the way, I discovered the fishbone analytical technique. I'm sure that at some point in the past, my version of the fishbone technique originated with the Ishikawa Cause and Effect Diagram, which graphs all causes or inputs for a particular effect, subdivided by category. I have freely adapted the technique for my own purposes, including preparing for speeches. It works well for me. It is a visual and spatial form of outlining your thoughts on any subject, only it is much more fun than an outline. The fishbone lets you think about issues in almost any sequence—a virtue that won't be lost on you if you have ever heard me give a speech. I used a fishbone to get organized for this book. (Here, my editor insists that this explains a lot, and adds that, for those who know what a *core dump* is in computer science parlance, the fishbone is Neal's way of producing one.) Like a core dump, the fishbone *is* a great way of getting all of your thoughts out of memory. The results, however, are much more navigable. As a tool for taking inventory of thoughts and solving problems, the fishbone is hard to beat.

For legibility reasons, I did not include one of my fishbone diagrams, but they are easy enough to create. First, take a clean sheet of paper and draw the backbone (a line) through the center of it. Make it an arrow going to the left. At the point of the arrow, write the result, objective, or solution to the business problem or opportunity. Add ribs connecting to the backbone, three or four per side, six to eight total. Now write at the top of the ribs the major categories of issues related to the problem or the work. Parse each rib into subissues, inputs, or tasks. If you are taking an inventory of ideas, keep subdividing until ideas stop flowing freely; if your goal is to solve a problem or improve a process, keep going until one clear solution or many potential improvements emerge.

At the end, you will see your thoughts in an organized fashion. And hopefully, you will also see the problem or opportunity through a more powerful lens. Like the four-box analysis, the fishbone is a framework upon which you can build your thoughts. Too many times, problems or opportunities are discussed without a means of encouraging a logical solution.

Small Groups: War Games, Think Weeks, & Work-Out Sessions

I love the problem-solving power of the small, energized group. It is critical for managers to develop the skills to lead discussion in a small group. Whenever possible, I like to have these sessions off campus, as the change in venue releases greater creativity leading to out-of-the-box solutions.

For years, I have convened, usually in my home and most often on Sunday evenings (it turns out the least disruptive to everyone's weekends), sessions I call War Games. Typically, these sessions deal with a single subject, and I make sure that the appropriate and empowered associates are present. I have found that those who know the facts and the ones responsible for the area are most often different people. The idea is to assemble the appropriate group of people to generate a healthy discussion, and then resolve together not to leave until a solution is reached.

I also use a day-long or multiday version of War Games for larger topics. For example, during the summer of 2004 we launched Lighthouse I and II at separate multi-day sessions at Grand Lake in Oklahoma. The basic rule is that we are using "live bullets"—that is to say, decisions made during the sessions will be executed Monday morning.

Usually one to three times a year, I have used what I call a Think Week to think through key business issues or to build entire business plans. This was a technique that I once read Bill Gates uses at Microsoft. I tried it more than 10 years ago and am a very strong believer in its power. These sessions have always created important changes in our direction as a company. The biggest issue is finding the available week. I find the time.

As CEO, I am responsible for our entire enterprise, so I take anywhere from a few days to a week, depending on the particular business issues or plans that need attention. If you are a team lead responsible for a more clearly defined part of Cerner, you are probably looking at calling a "Think Day". While our scopes are different, you will find that this technique scales. If you cannot find a day between Monday morning and Friday evening, try Saturday.

Not too long ago, we instituted a methodology for driving business improvements called Work-Out, a discipline developed by Jack Welch at GE. One of the things I really like about the Work-Out process is that it is a more formal, therefore repeatable, process based on many of the same things that have made War Games and Think Week work for me. It adds the discipline of a powerful set of analytics as a prerequisite for holding the sessions.

The key driver behind all of these ideas is the power of a small group of the right people to solve problems or plan opportunities.

Do the Math

I am hard wired to do the math—to identify and compute the basic facts and figures associated with an organization, its resources, and its profitability. It is a habit that helps me start at the end as an executive. I am shocked that many managers do not attempt to build an overall framework for solving problems or making decisions by doing simple math. Managers who do not build such a framework are more likely to become confused with the details associated with viewing their responsibilities and challenges from the limited perspective of what looks and feels right. It is important not to overlook the factual story told by numbers.

One of our more significant challenges today is overall productivity in all segments of Cerner. We manage one of the largest healthcare information consultancies in the world. When I approach this subject, I go to the board and do the math.

Do the Math

In 2003, here was my math:

- 2,000 associates in Cerner Consulting X 2,000 hours per year
- 4,000,000 hours paid for @ 80% chargeable ratio
- 3,200,000 billable hours X $150 per hour
- $480,000,000 Expected Revenue

Figure 2.8 – Do the Math 2003

Figure 2.8 is a slide I presented to Cerner leaders in 2003 when challenging them to think about the math. Actual revenue was less than $300,000,000. I expect to be working with executives who can tell me what happened to the shareholders' $180,000,000.

Figure 2.9 is a slide from a more recent quarterly forecast meeting. It includes math from the second quarter of 2004.

Do the Math 2004

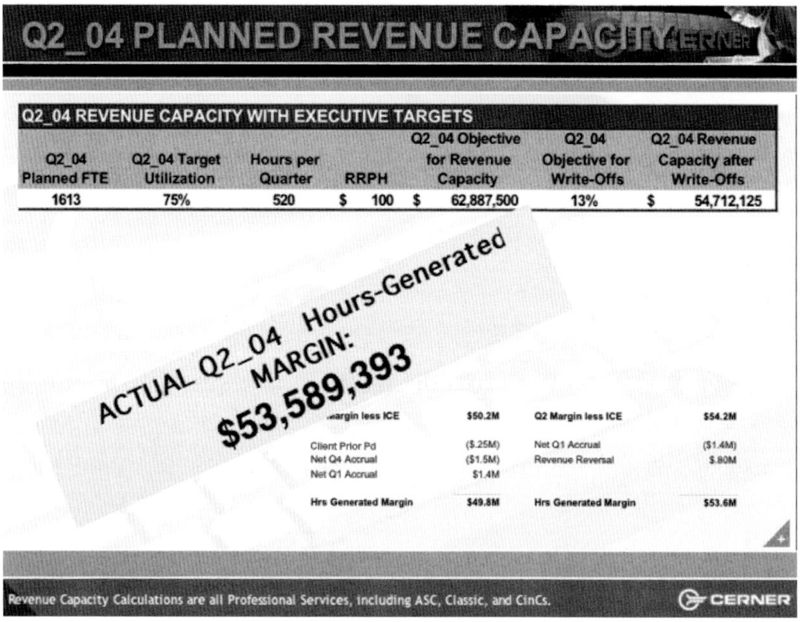

Figure 2.9 – Do the Math 2004

Do the math. Know your numbers. Did you notice that the above chart uses a different chargeable ratio and hourly rate than I did in my 2003 example? I did! A corollary to do the math: Check the math.

****

As promised, this chapter was about my personal techniques for approaching the job of management, not about the act of managing. Now, let's proceed to making *manage* a dynamic verb.

Chapter Three

Plan, Execute, & Control

Planning is bringing the future into the present
so that you can do something about it now.
– Alan Lakein

I said before that *managers manage* (a dynamic verb), and that management is a full-contact sport. Part of what makes managing so dynamic is that, in many cases, you as a manager must both manage and do. You are on the field as both player and coach. Clients, associates, and others will all need decisions. You must make these decisions quickly and confidently and set direction for others. You are responsible for delivering business results that bring value to clients. You will be held accountable. In this chapter, I will present the most basic actions you are responsible for as a manager:

- *To* plan *how your team will achieve a goal or objective*

- *To* execute *the plan to produce the planned results*

- *To have a system of* controls *that allows you to quickly identify when results vary from the plan, to explain the variance, and to take corrective action*

All three actions—plan, execute, and control—are essential. You probably advanced in your career because you were good at *doing*. Perhaps, like most people, you prefer to just get moving on something—anything. Don't fall into this trap. Without a plan, there is no control, only execution. Execution without control is assumed to be out of control, and being out of control is always a management problem. Producing business results against a plan is the essence of your role as a manager. "Missing plan" is bad. It creates a ripple of consequences that can cause harm to the entire organization. Exceeding a plan also causes rework for others, so you should never sandbag. Be honest, plan wisely, and then do everything in your power to execute the plan and control its results.

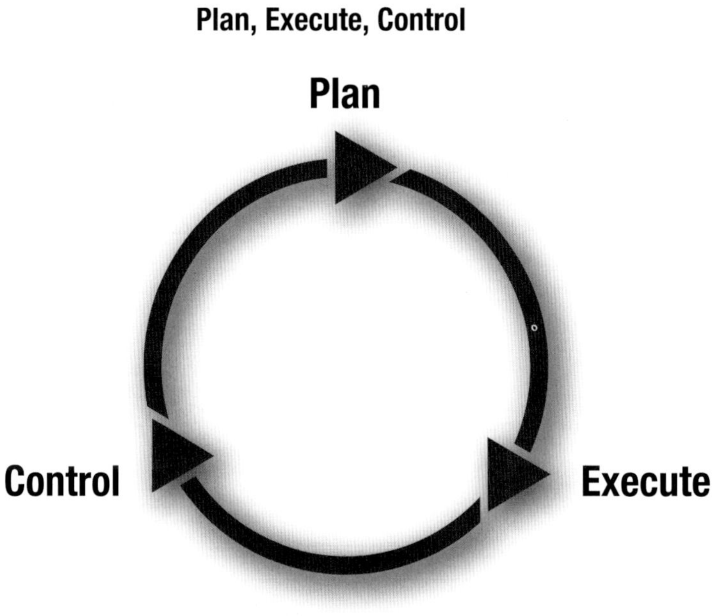

Plan, Execute, Control

Plan

Control   **Execute**

Figure 3.1 – Plan, Execute, & Control

To Plan

The vision is clear, you know your mission as a manager, and the strategies have been set. As a manager, you are responsible for getting from point A to point B. Now you plan.

To plan is to address the basic questions of who, what, when, and where about a set of activities that are essential to a desired result. When you plan, you set concrete goals and measurable objectives for your team, and you determine the right structure, process, tools, and effort to accomplish them. A good plan creates clarity for everyone on the team regarding *what* result is expected, *when* it is expected, *by whom* it is to be produced, and *where* it is to be done. A good manager makes sure that the entire team also knows *why* the plan must be done, otherwise it is just a work order.

A plan must include goals that are clear to everyone, and objectives that can and will be measured. Goals and objectives are the specific statements of the results you want to attain. A *goal* is a general statement of a desired result, for example, "Improve the client experience." An *objective* further refines the goal into a measurable result by a certain point in time: "In 2005, improve client survey results by five percent for all community hospital clients." For any specific goal, several objectives may be defined. *Managers manage* to objectives.

You must plan both the operational and financial performance of your organization. Both must be integrated with Cerner's corporate operational and financial master plan. The 2005 corporate financial plan has at its base over 180 individual unit plans from each of the major business units in our corporate structure. At the top of our corporate plan is our business model. As a business manager, it is important that you understand how your business unit fits into Cerner's business model. In the Cerner 2003 Annual Report, we published a basic primer on how the Cerner business model works. This was for shareholders to better understand the "levers" that impact our margin and performance. You need to understand these levers, because, as managers, it is your hands that pull them. You must make sure that your team also understands our business model. At one of your staff meetings, review with your team how their results fit into Cerner's overall model of business.

Unless you are a very senior executive, chances are you will need to synchronize a minimum of three plans: One is the plan you create for your team or project; another is the plan your own manager has created for his or her part of the organization; a third is Cerner's corporate master plan. In essence, all are the same plan, but each layer goes into greater precision about who, what, where, and when results will be produced. Your manager's plan sets parameters for your plan. These parameters can be broad—"Develop a profitable new business segment in under a year"— or they can be specific—"Convert 12 new referenceable CPOE client sites in Cerner West by the end of third quarter." Either way, you are still responsible for creating *your* plan and synchronizing it with others, complete with specific goals for the associates who work for you.

Logic dictates that the company's overall operational and financial plans should be developed from the bottom up. After all, the whole must be the sum of the parts. I have a confession to make: I do not believe that plans can be developed from the bottom up. My belief has come through hard-earned experience. I find it works better to define the overall goals and objectives from the top down, including how much Cerner will invest in each area of the company. When plans are developed from the bottom up, there is almost always a compounding effect in the padding of expectations that ultimately is unfeasible, and often even nonsensical, when summed up and up to the company level. In fact, the performance of the individual unit plans should add up to a greater total than the corporate performance to adjust for inevitable variance in performance that each of the units will have.

While offering confessions, I will share another strong belief: There should be two plans developed. The first one I call our "financial plan". It represents our conservative view of the year. This is the one we use to drive our resource commitment and spending across Cerner. We *hire and spend* to this plan. As a public company, we share portions of this plan with "the Street". We have a lot of confidence in achieving it, both financially and operationally. The second plan is a "stretch plan". It is achievable, but more things must go right to achieve it. The stretch plan should be the one used as the management plan. We use both plans to determine our variable compensation plans.

Planning is hard. When I hear the word *hope* from a manager, or hear it used in a business context, it is an immediate flag to me that either there is NO plan or that the current plan has failed. In making a plan, you are committing to deliver future results. Many others in our organization are counting on you to make your plan because of the impact it will have on their plans. To plan correctly, you must be able to model the future at a very detailed level. You will make a number of assumptions in building the plan. The quality of your plan will reside in your ability to identify, assess, and declare these assumptions. A couple of examples of the types of assumptions you might have to make include the availability of the next release and the sales mix of bookings (license versus services). The list gets very long.

As a manager making a plan, you have constraints. Understand the variables and constraints of your plan. Your manager's plan and the corporate plan are demanding. You will not have all the resources you want. You will not have all of the time you want. You will not control your environments. Clients will do things you do not expect. Competitors will try to make you fail. Associates above you and below you will disappoint you.

Your tendency will be predictable. The above constraints will confuse you. You will want to use the current year to prepare for future years, deferring making your financial plan for this year. You will delay finalizing the plan until the period is over. After all, it is easier to plan the past. It is easier to be accurate.

Even in the face of this tendency (_especially_ in the face of this tendency), you must always have a plan. Without one, how will you be accountable for any results? How will you know whether you are behind or ahead? There is NO excuse for not having a plan. No matter how inadequate you may feel to predict the future, you have a responsibility to attempt it. You were chosen for your position, in part, because someone thought you were more qualified than the rest of the field to do precisely this. Give your plan as much detail as possible, and react quickly as you watch it unfold. Over time, you will get better at planning.

Plan vs. Forecast and Budget

A couple of comments on two related terms, _forecast_ and _budget_, that many people want to use interchangeably with the word _plan_. First, the word _forecast_. **Forecasts are not plans.** They are snapshots of key variables that are vital to your plan. I cringe when I hear managers use the terms _forecast_ and _plan_ interchangeably. Saying, "But I made my forecast!" is clear evidence that the manager either lacks management skill or does not have a plan. Making a forecast is an extremely useful management process for control, especially if that forecast exceeds the plan for that period. A good forecast process involves much of the organization and is driven from the *bottom up*. We have for some time produced a forecast of our contract bookings and system conversions every 90 days. While the greatest attention is given to the upcoming quarter, we actually forecast the next four quarters, thereby producing a running view of our next year. Most of the sales staff will forecast what deals they will close this quarter. These predictions are rolled up into different views and ultimately are summarized for the entire company. The senior management team will review each person's (producer's) contribution and will risk-adjust the forecast. This is an extremely valuable process, but it does not replace the plan. The plan does not change because we forecast. Forecasts change daily. Plans do not. Only managers plan. As managers, we may change our plans based on forecasts. The two processes, however, are entirely different. Do not confuse them.

Second in the short list of words that should not be confused with *plan* is the word *budget*. At Cerner, we plan; we do not budget. Budgets are for home and for bureaucrats. A budget is planned spending. At Cerner, we do not plan to spend; we plan to produce results. You will need to invest some of Cerner's resources to get there, which will be in your plan.

To Execute

To execute is to put your plan into effect. Execution is hard work.

In a perfect world, your plan would go off without a hitch. Everyone on the team would do what they're supposed to do, processes would flow, tools would work, environments would cooperate, estimates would be accurate, clients would "ooh", deadlines would be met, and executives would be beaming. I don't want to depress or surprise you, but things rarely occur this easily.

Much of execution is making decisions when the inevitable problems arise. You will be trying to predict the future. The solutions won't be so clear. In reality, you will never have all the data you want or need to know that you have made the right decision. The higher you are in the company, the greater the degree of uncertainty. Expect problems, and do not lose focus or commitment to your plan when the problems occur. Think. Use problem-solving techniques. Ask for advice from your manager, peer group, or mentors. Whatever you do, make the decision required to move your team forward. Do not let a lack of _your_ decision-making delay anyone else's execution. Know the triggers that will require you to make adjustments to the plan. **_The art of management is making timely and quality decisions in the face of ambiguity._**

If you manage a project of any type—software development, client engagement, or creative—execution also means starting strong and knowing when you are finished. A huge mistake I see is starting too quickly without getting the project organized. Another is overplanning and not getting started quickly enough. At the beginning of a project, there is less pressure and everyone thinks there is plenty of time. I learned many years ago that the key to meeting deadlines is in the first half of the project, not the heroics at conversion or at the deadline. Finishing, too, is hard because there is an awkward phase at the end when it's difficult to know if the project is complete. Scope is usually very fluid at the end. **_The art of project management is in starting and...finishing._**

Once you have completed your plan, you need to distribute it within your organization. Define the critical path and make sure that everyone knows his or her role and part in making or breaking the project. If people do not know your expectations, they cannot be expected to meet them. Execution means making sure that everyone on your team knows at all times what the plan is, whether the team is currently on track to achieve the desired results, and what they personally have to do today to make the plan succeed. Do not underestimate the need to prioritize tasks for *every* member on your team, including our clients and business partners. A talented associate is soon inundated with requests too numerous to fulfill; make sure this associate knows which tasks are mission-critical. Beware if your team members are not dedicated to your plan full time. They will quickly be confused about who sets their priorities.

Execution also means motivating and inspecting. Make sure you are communicating enough on both the group and individual level to understand what your team members want and need to succeed. Ask each person to demonstrate what they are doing to meet their objectives. *The science of project management is in setting and enforcing expectations. The effective project manager makes sure that every project member knows each day what they must do before they go home—and they do it.*

Execution is also creating clarity about the current status of your plan to your own manager and executive. If your plan begins to fail, your manager should know about it before the situation is unrecoverable. No one likes to deliver or receive bad news, but everyone *hates surprises.* Your manager has skills and experience that may help you, but she or he will need honest reporting from you to understand and mitigate the business issues that will arise from your unplanned variance. Update your managers with succinct but meaningful reports of your real results, trends, and progress. Always live by a policy of "no surprises".

At the end of the day, your value to the company and to our clients will be in your ability to consistently deliver results through execution. As a manager, your reputation will be determined most succinctly through your ability to deliver results. You have to take this responsibility personally.

To Control

To control is to compare actual results against planned results as they emerge, and to take corrective action, when necessary, to improve results or get your plan back on track.

Measurement

Control implies having a measurement system in place from the start. *Without measurement, there can be no management.* Without measurement, you will have no frame of reference through which to impose control. So, once you have carefully defined the desired result in the planning phase, make sure you are in a position to measure it. Be careful in choosing your short-term metrics. Your measurements must be sensitive to the operational and financial objectives in both your unit plan and Cerner's quarterly and annual plan. At the end of the quarter or year, will your metrics really correspond to operational and financial success in your plan? Cerner managers are expected to know the difference between "counting" and relevant measurement. A relevant measurement is sensitive to some desired business result. For example, Cash Receipts, while very important, is a count of dollars received. Days Sales Outstanding (DSO), on the other hand, is a measurement that is sensitive to both the current balance of Accounts Receivables *and* Revenues. Ask any Wall Street analyst which one is more important to measuring the financial performance of a company. (Hint: DSO.) You must develop measurements that are sensitive to your mission.

The value of results must be inherent in the measurement. One of the oldest forms of business measurement is a Profit and Loss (P&L) statement— with success being defined as revenues greater than expenses. My favorite standard measurement is the Cash Flow statement. As a manager, you should be able to read and understand all of the traditional accounting statements. The big three are Balance Sheet, P&L, and Cash Flow.

Once a measurement system is in place, the active part of controlling the plan begins. The first part of active control is to use your measurement system to compare the attainment of actual results, trend them across time periods, and measure their variance from planned results and previous results. At every step in the plan, study the variances between expected and actual results, and make sure that, as manager, you know what the root causes of these variances are. At all times, you must be able to explain variances from the plan in clear language.

Inspection

The second part of active control is inspecting. In the same sense that you cannot manage what you do not measure, you should never *expect* what you do not *inspect*. Inspection, therefore, is a form of execution that can impact the plan and is necessary for control. Inspection involves meeting with the team members or team leaders, and reviewing the measurements and their attainment. The inspection process helps you bond with your team and allows you to understand the underlying activities driving performance.

Is the team meeting the measure at the expense of other variables (no investment, associate morale, and so on)? Inspections should happen on a recurrent basis and should be expected by your team. It shows you are engaged and part of their success. If the inspection goes well, then everyone understands the team is on track to achieve success, and they continue to execute. When inspection shows underlying problems, you are responsible to "go deep" with the team, understand the situation, and correct the course. Problems do not get better with age. The sooner you can work with your team, the less severe the impact on your team and the broader Cerner team will be. The algorithm in the next chapter, "From Vision to Value", should give you a better idea of how and what to inspect in your plan.

Correction

The third aspect of active control is taking corrective action. It is an accident if your results are exactly what you planned! There is always variance, because your plan will never be an exact model of reality. Study the variance, and understand why it is occurring or what assumptions in the original plan were wrong.

Spend some quality time determining your response to the variance. Sometimes, the variance will be small and you will do nothing. Many times, you will adjust how you are executing against the plan. On certain rare occasions, you will find it is necessary to stop and build a new plan. I call this a replan. Knowing when to do a replan takes some practice and wisdom. It should not be undertaken lightly. You are responsible for DELIVERING RESULTS. Do not change your original plan often. Do change how you are executing when you are failing to meet the plan.

There will be times when you are significantly exceeding the original plan. Keep it up, but think through the downstream consequences this surplus may produce. During some of our company's periods of fastest growth, exceeding plan also required us to replan several key elements of our original plan, including the hiring and investing portions. A much less exciting circumstance is when you are significantly underperforming against the plan, and the underperformance will produce dire consequences. Usually this is caused by creating a poor original plan, one in which some major assumptions were grossly miscalculated. Other times the original plan is good, but very poor execution causes poor results, such as a failure to carry out the proper timing or quality of a major release.

One of the bigger challenges you will face as a manager is how to control factors in your plan that are seemingly outside of your control. Your success or failure depends on other teams or people, other physical things, other results. On a daily basis, you will be asked to rely on the judgment of another manager, the cooperation of a domain, the "art" of software development, the whim of a client. In many cases, your control comes from your persuasiveness and your determination to overcome any obstacle. Persuade and conquer. Your ability to describe the challenges, benefits, and incentives of a given situation, and your relentlessness in pursuing fixes to any problem, will determine your success. It is impossible to overemphasize the importance of understanding what motivates *other* people to solve problems *for you*. The manager who understands persuasion has won half of the battles already.

Realistically, there will be times in your career as a manager when factors in your internal or external environment change in such a way that it now *seems impossible* to achieve the results set out in the original plan.

Persuasion and persistence aren't going to do it. Maybe your team is just flat-out unable to do the work they estimated they could do. Perhaps another manager missed his or her plan, and your plan is entirely dependent on it. Perhaps the overall landscape changes in a dramatic way because of a wildcard force at work: a competitor's innovation, a breakthrough technology, a legal hurdle, a regulatory change. These types of occurrences unfortunately are common in business. Remember, managers manage. Some of our greatest innovations come from the pressure of knowing the results we need to achieve, but not knowing how to achieve them. So think twice—no, think _three_ times—before giving up on achieving your plan. Innovate. Invent. Inspire. Change the definition of what is in your control. There will be no limits to your career if you get a reputation for achieving results when everything around you is crumbling.

But what if you have allowed yourself and other smart people the opportunity to think about the problem, and you still can't come up with a solution? The answer will depend on the severity of the problem. For some problems, the right answer might be for you to _propose_ minor adjustments to the scope, resources, or timing of your plan. This will require the input of your own manager, your clients, and sometimes even your executive management team. Although it is uncomfortable to ask for such changes, as long as the logic behind your proposal is sound, you should find your request met with approval. It will help if you articulate what you have already thought of or tried.

On certain occasions, the damage is too severe or the change in your environment too abrupt for a minor plan adjustment to work. Under these circumstances, you're best off admitting that it's time to _replan_. Replanning is a big deal. Replanning means changing the fundamental assumptions about what results will be achieved, and building a new plan to go after these results. As a manager, you don't want to be *known* for having to replan, but it's 100 times better to pull off a proactive replan than to sit helplessly by while your original plan goes up in flames.

Measuring, inspecting, adjusting, persuading, innovating, reevaluating, and replanning are examples of *control* in the face of varying degrees of obstacles. Being in control is the opposite of being a victim. When we make our plans, we have to plan for the fair, reasonable, and expected to occur; but we *also* have to plan for the *unfair, unreasonable*, and *unexpected*. As managers, we have to create our own luck.

Plan, Execute, & Control for Executives

I want to add a few thoughts for executives who are managing a series of interlocking and multiyear plans. First, if the plan extends across several quarters, you will need to adjust—guaranteed. Know the trigger events that require you to rethink and calibrate your plan. This could be the signing or merely the possibility of signing a major contract that was not in the current plan. Also anticipate the turns in the road ahead, new legislation that impacts the cash flow of our clients, the loss of a key executive, or the entry of a new competitor. The road is never straight for long. Knowing this and anticipating this are executive attributes.

Second, it is possible to deliver your results, but still fail your plan. As you manage to the plan, you will have variances against different parts of your plan. Sometimes it will be possible to compensate for a loss in one part of a plan with a gain in another. In a financial plan, for example, if you expected the Services part of your business to perform in a certain way, but it is operating below plan, you still have the ability to adjust other levers in your business model to make your objective. Your ability to understand the variables and adjust your actions might even allow you to obtain the financial results intended in the original plan. The wise executive treats an outcome like this the same as a failure, and delivers the inspection and explanation that are due. While lever-pulling may work for a period in a financial plan, the definition of success is often stricter in an operational plan.

And finally, do not game the plan. Unfortunately, the recent corporate landscape is filled with organizations that seemingly delivered significant plan attainment, but did so through intentional obfuscation of the true business results (HBOC, Enron, and Tyco are modern-day examples). In the end, these corrupt plans unraveled to the detriment of these executives and their enterprises. Other organizations achieved short-term results without properly investing for future success (for example, commercial airline union contracts, AT&T selling off wireless, and AOL in broadband). If you are making the plan by underinvesting in new development or new associates, or by artificial actions that cannot be sustained, you are doing yourself, your associates, and Cerner a disservice. There is no excuse for a manager who makes his or her plan one year, but misses the following year because he or she failed to invest in new markets, grow new associates, or invest properly in infrastructure. Corrective action means acknowledging and addressing underlying issues and not mortgaging future performance.

****

Plan, execute, and control. As managers, these verbs define our fundamental responsibilities.

———————— CHAPTER THREE ————————

In the next chapter, I will share with you a formula and sequence of thought that should help you *plan* more completely, *execute* your plans, and inspect and *control* plans that are not producing results. When understood and done correctly, the actions of planning, executing, and controlling should become inseparable—sustaining and balancing each other.

Chapter Four

From Vision to Value

Vision without action is merely a dream.
Action without vision just passes the time.
Vision with action can change the world.
– Joel A. Barker

The management actions I described in the previous chapter—*plan, execute,* and *control*—are a traditional view of management responsibilities. Some time ago, I developed a simple algorithm that I use to create a larger context and sequence to managing and leading as Cerner's chief executive. I believe it is applicable down to the most focused business units and smallest of teams. For decades, I have used the algorithm as a reminder of the elements an organization or individual plan requires to be successful.

During the summer of 1979, Paul Gorup, Cliff Illig, and I spent our Sunday mornings in Loose Park in Kansas City, at a picnic table discussing and planning what is now called Cerner Corporation. I made the leap first to leave Arthur Andersen's consulting organization (now Accenture) late that July, and my last day of employment at Andersen was September 3rd, 1979. One evening later that week, the three of us, all in our twenties, sat around my dining room table assessing whether Cliff and Paul would join me in this new venture. We were playing it by ear. We had no manual to reference or experience to tell us what to do. In the beginning of any new venture, your instincts control you, and the dominant instinct is survival. It was clear that the journey was going to be a lot of trial and error, but *too big* of an error would end our endeavor quickly. Along this amazing journey,

I continually pursued the answer to the question, "What does a real executive do?" Over the first decade, the vast number of essential responsibilities the executive must manage gradually distilled into categories. I developed a way of using these categories in a management algorithm, describing their relationships and sequence. I have tested it a number of times, and I have a strong belief in it. It is easily adaptable to a whole company, a small team, or any organization in between.

What follows is a description of the sequence and variables in the Vision-to-Value (V^2) algorithm.

Vision-to-Value (V^2) Algorithm

$$\text{Vision} + \text{Mission} + \text{Strategy} + \text{Structure} + \text{Process} + \text{Tools}$$
$$= \text{Results (Attainment, Trend, Variance)}$$

Figure 4.1 – Vision-to-Value (V^2 Algorithm)

Vision: Creating Purpose for the Journey

One of the boldest visions expressed in the twentieth century was John F. Kennedy's articulation of the idea of going to the moon. On May 25, 1961, President Kennedy said in a special address to Congress that, "…this nation should commit itself to achieving the goal, before this decade is out, of landing a man on the moon and returning him safely to earth. No single space project in this period will be more exciting, or more impressive, or more important for the long-range exploration of space; and none will be so difficult or expensive to accomplish."

Vision is the articulation of a future state. It is both a purpose and a destination for the organization. A good vision is one that is understandable and believable but, at the same time, is beyond our current understanding of *how* to achieve it. Even though vision does not declare the exact *when*, vision must be achievable within a conceivable time frame. Five to 15 years is good for many human endeavors. Vision should tax but ultimately be within the reach of your organization's capabilities.

In addition to being within reach, vision must be both insightful and compelling. I have often said, ***"The art of vision is connecting the dots."*** A *dot* is a salient fact or event capable of affecting the future state. Everyone is capable of seeing the dots; relatively few individuals have the insight or instinct to connect them. Connecting the dots is a metaphor for the ability to find the key relationships, and the patterns that the relationships draw, that will create fundamental change of the present state to a new future state. The anticipated state presented in the vision must be truly compelling, something that offers convincing reasons to warrant achievement. In the case of JFK's vision in 1961, the Soviets then had a clear lead on the United States in space technology. There was a broad belief that if the U.S. and its allies lost the space race, we would lose the Cold War. The prospect of losing the Cold War and risking Soviet domination, combined with aspirations of pioneering progress in space exploration, compelled the United States to pursue JFK's vision.

Vision has at least three major functions in an organization. First, vision can serve as the ultimate *alignment* technique. If we all have the same destination in mind as a management team, we are very likely to collaborate by making decisions that support and complement each other. Second, vision creates *purpose* for the journey. There is nothing more motivating for an organization than to be given a clear purpose, and nothing more meaningful as a manager than to provide it. Lastly, leading through vision is how you *move the boundaries* of an organization, the ultimate organic growth strategy.

Cerner's history demonstrates how we have used our vision to expand our boundaries and grow as a company. In the beginning, Cerner was created on the concept of "investing in building information technology that automated the core mission-critical processes of an information-driven industry." While we did not call this our vision, it defined the conceptual framework for our startup. In 1979, probably 90 percent of the computer systems that were in use in healthcare had their genesis as financial and administrative systems. They were not engineered for the real mission of healthcare. Our first focus, laboratory medicine, was mission-critical to our clients, at least in our eyes. If the clinical laboratory in a major medical center is out of service, it forces the closure of surgery and completely cripples the physician's ability to diagnose and monitor therapies of the sickest patients. The clinical laboratory is not the center of healthcare, but it is the *nexus* of healthcare. Cerner's focus has been mission-critical from the beginning.

By late 1984, the dots were connecting in my mind. First, as only a laboratory company, our growth would slow substantially by the end of the decade. Keep in mind that Cerner was still an infant in 1984; and our first system, *PathNet* laboratory information system, was far from complete. Second, hospitals were organized internally as silos and clearly needed a method of coordinating care. Third, key relationships existed in the data generated inside the silos that, under a common architecture, would be extremely powerful in improving the quality and safety of clinical medicine. Calculating the dose of a drug, for example, requires laboratory data about how well the kidneys function. Fourth and finally, all of the silos used a common set of functions in their care of patients (registration, ordering, results viewing, management reporting, and so on). Each of these functions had to be replicated in each of the stand-alone or best-of-breed applications. The bigger healthcare financial systems companies—SMS, McDonnell Douglas, and HBOC—did not understand clinical systems; to them, that was where charges came from. We moved the boundary of our image from Cerner, the laboratory system company, to become Cerner, the clinical system company. *Health Network Architecture (HNA)* was born.

In *HNA*, I learned the importance of moving the boundaries, but I also learned how difficult it is to change the culture of an organization. The easy part is to connect the dots and communicate your epiphany excitedly. I learned firsthand, however, how unbelievably difficult it is to change the mindset of an entire organization to understand and believe in a new vision. In some sense, you are trying to convince a trout to become a salmon. In the mid-1980s, the language, the image, and the identity of our company were those of a laboratory company, not of a clinical company. It was a real struggle to alter the company's perception of its own identity. If we had not prevailed, our company would not have changed, and ultimately we would have become food for the larger fish in the ocean. If you as a manager and leader are trying to change your organization, you have to be very persistent in pursuing your vision and looking for ways to make it more real to your team.

I made the point in the beginning of this book that I am communicating lessons learned. Lessons learned do not necessarily constitute hard science. That does not mean, however, that there is no real empirical evidence behind my thoughts. In 1980, the two major players in the laboratory information systems (LIS) business were MedLab, which was at that time a division of Control Data Corporation, and CHC, a private, Houston-based LIS company. Today they are both gone—fish food. By the end of the

1980s, our competitors were Sunquest, Terrano Lab, Rubicon, and Citation. Today, all are gone—also fish food. Cerner over the years acquired the remains of some of these long-term competitors. Sunquest lasted for the entire decade of the 1990s but never really became anything other than an LIS company, even though they tried to emulate nearly everything we did. How do you explain Cerner's continued success over a three-decade period? Some might say that we were smarter. But I do not believe we were that much (if at all) smarter. We learned the importance of vision early—and we never forgot it.

The broad vision statement, *To Automate the Process of Managing Healthcare*, guided us for many years. Today, in the absence of context, that vision sounds almost bland, but I assure you that it was radical when the then-present was dominated by stand-alone departmental systems built to get the bill out. As we actually began to automate the processes of healthcare in the early 1990s, the vision statement became more of a mission statement. If you achieve the vision, then it is no longer vision. The slide in Figure 4.2 is an artifact from one of my slide decks. Its vintage is early 1990s. I used it to show how our boundaries expanded between 1980 and 1995, and to create the case for building *HNA Millennium* (originally called *version 500*—I played a word game with *vision* and *version*).

The numbers 100 through 400 refer to versions of architecture known today as *Cerner Classic*. From the beginning, Cerner was unique in believing that the best practice of medicine depended on the free flow of information across a single information architecture, with the patient as its focus rather than the department, the physician, or the patient's bill. By 1993, however, our expanding vision of *HNA* was being constrained by our technological platform. A growing number of clients believed in the concept of a single architecture and its focus on the patient rather

Moving the Boundaries

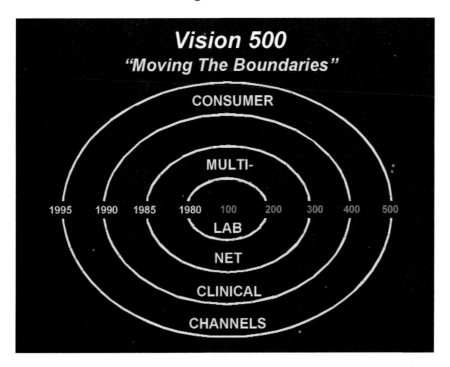

Figure 4.2 – Moving the Boundaries

than the bill. Our thinking had evolved, though, and by then we were absolutely convinced that the logical information center for the practice of medicine was the *person*, from the moment of conception to the moment of death, in illness and in health, and in healthcare contexts from the operating room to the living room. Anything else, even the *patient*, was a compromise. A new person-centered architecture would mean better care for the individual and would allow us to create a feedback loop that could improve the practice of medicine in the future. In version 500 we were going to make the major shift that would allow us to build the relational data model this vision demanded. Before it was completed, *version 500* became known as *HNA Millennium. Note: In 2001,*

Cerner's marketing group officially dropped all references to HNA and changed the name to Cerner Millennium. I have always liked what HNA stands for, so I reserve my old-timers' privilege to use it from time to time.

The higher you climb, the farther you can see. Our vision continued to broaden. By the mid-1990s, Cerner's concept of the *person* expanded to include communities and populations. We started communicating and even identifying our vision with this picture we called the Community Health Model:

Community Health Model

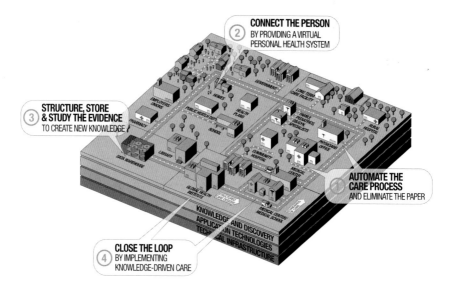

Figure 4.3 – The Community Health Model

To date, our vision has evolved from the laboratory, to clinical systems, to the medical enterprise, to the community, and now to the health economy, addressing the systemic issues of health and healthcare at the country level. In 2005, we are actively engaged in improving healthcare for a country of more than 50 million people, and we are realistically

The Second 25 Years

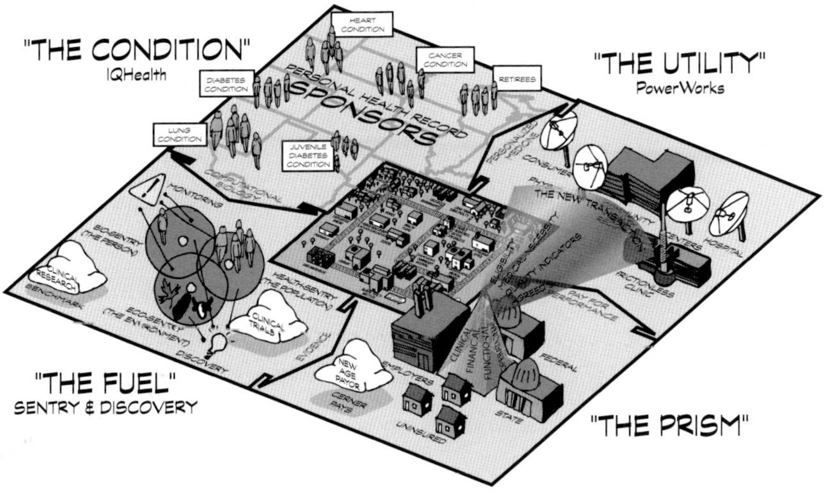

Figure 4.4 – The Second 25 Years

envisioning ways to vitalize health economies around the world. We recently unveiled a new Community Health Model image to help communicate this further extension of our vision (Figure 4.4).

Over the years, most of our beliefs have stayed constant; we have just taken a successively broader view of the same core issues. At Cerner, envisioning bold solutions to the systemic flaws and challenges of the healthcare system gives each of us a purpose for our work.

If you need more proof of the importance of vision, consider the fact that vision has driven our organic growth for more than two decades. Nearly all of our growth from zero to $1 billion in revenues has been organic growth associated with expanding our solutions and markets in pursuit of our vision. As our vision has evolved from only laboratory early on to the entire health economy today, the opportunity for organic growth has increased. I'm not sure what the total size of the United States laboratory market was in

1985, but the health economy in the United States in 2003 was $1.5 trillion. If we have the most powerful value proposition in the healthcare industry, then we have the opportunity, subject to our leadership and management skills, to continue to grow Cerner significantly.

Making a visionary transformation creates the opportunity for a company to grow. We grew 100 times from 1985 to 2005 (estimated), from $10 million to more than $1 billion in revenues. What is 100 times $1 billion? You now know part of the reason I was compelled to introduce an expansion of our company vision at the fall 2004 Town Hall meeting and Cerner Health Conference. The vision element is the only element in the V^2 algorithm that embeds such tremendous organic growth opportunities.

Vision comes before everything else. As a manager, you are responsible for, at bare minimum, *communicating* Cerner's vision to your team. As a leader or executive, you also should be *setting* the vision for your team. You should be connecting the dots in your environment and looking ahead to a future others can't see. Your unique perspective can add richness and dimension to your manager's vision and Cerner's enterprise vision. Everyone in the organization will benefit if you lay out a world-changing but conceivable vision for your team.

Be sure the vision doesn't stop with you. The power of vision is creating a shared vision with our clients and associates. This happens only if you have a vision, communicate it, and make it real in people's minds.

Mission: Action the Vision

Mission is the actionable and achievable extension of the vision. In day-to-day activities, I have always blurred the two intentionally. The two variables are very similar, with the mission being actionable and repeatable. Mission is a clear direction required to create the future state described by the vision. Mission requires more frequent adjustment than vision; I suggest every three to five years.

As with vision, mission can come in the form of a brief and broad corporate statement—*To connect the appropriate person(s), resources, and knowledge at the proper time and location to achieve the optimal health outcome*— or in the form of a detailed picture, such as this one describing the bundling of our technology into solutions:

Application Map

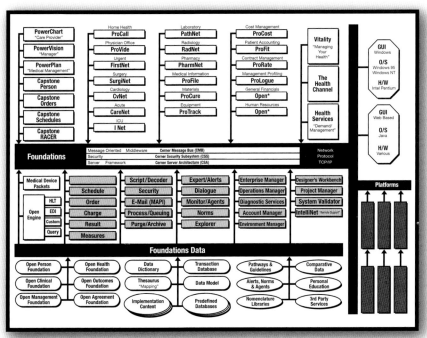

Figure 4.5 – Application Map, circa late 1990's

The application map in Figure 4.5 has been in use at Cerner since the early 1990s. It has gone through a number of revisions, but clients, investors, and associates appreciate its concrete nature to describe something as broad, abstract, and intricate as *Cerner Millennium*.

As a manager, you should consider creating or refreshing the mission statement for your organization or team. Strive to keep the mission clear by sharing roadmaps and other visual aids that show where you are going.

Strategies: Big Decisions, Clever Paths

I have taught myself, "If you are making tough choices, you are possibly creating strategy."

Strategy involves choice of a major pathway for the company or engagement. You simply cannot go down every road. Some of the most anxious moments in your professional life will come when you are defining strategies. There is a sense of loss and risk in choosing paths. Most of the angst is an awareness of the fact that if you are wrong, it will be very costly. Just imagine what would have happened if *Cerner Millennium* had failed. It's simple. The predators would have struck—Cerner would have become fish food.

Strategy follows mission. If you are developing a strategy and have not defined the mission, then either you are lost, or you will be soon.

A note about strategy and tactics: In military usage, strategies are the overall, large-scale, and long-term plans for winning the war or accomplishing other major objectives. In many cases, strategy is conducted off the field, prior to engaging in a particular battle. Tactics are specific learned techniques (such as flanking and maneuvers) used to get the job done once the specific battlefield is defined.

In business, a strategy is a statement of the desired pathway a company, group, or individual manager plans to take to achieve vision, mission, goals, and objectives. For example, One Architecture (*Health Network Architecture*) was—and remains—a strategy of using a single, common architectural platform to achieve Cerner's vision and mission. Strategies are inherently creative, depend on analysis of likely future events, and always involve a choice. Successful strategies create competitive advantage.

Tactics implement strategy; they define how to move down the strategic pathway. Tactics are learned, repeatable, and established techniques. The outcome of a tactic relies less on creativity and wisdom than it does on skillful execution and individual prowess. Once you come up with a strategy, you choose tactics based on all the assets and options at your disposal. Your *plan* is a roll-up of all the tactics you will use to deliver the results anticipated by your vision, mission, and strategy.

While they are usually easy to distinguish from one another, occasionally the lines between strategy and tactics blur. One of my favorite examples of this blurring is the story of Tom Monaghan, his brother James, and their restaurant, Domino's Pizza. Their original vision and mission were for the single Domino's to be a stand-alone Italian restaurant that featured pizza. Tom wanted only enough money to pay for his college tuition. Business was so bad, however, that for the sake of stimulating the necessary cash flow to keep the doors open, they *tactically* decided to deliver pizza to their customers. James saw the writing on the wall and traded his half of the restaurant to Tom for a used Volkswagen Beetle. The rest is history. Today they have more than 7,500 restaurants. Home delivery, the tactic to keep cash flowing, became the strategy that transformed the industry.

I mentioned that strategies always involve a choice. In the case of the One Architecture strategy, we made a conscious choice to develop all Cerner solutions using a common data model so that information could be shared on the back end without interfaces. An alternate strategy would have been to develop or acquire stand-alone departmental solutions and interface their resulting data (a strategy most of our competitors chose). Our strategy, as with all choices, has a number of drawbacks or *costs:*

1. *New solutions must be developed within an existing technological framework, restricting some avenues of development.*

2. *Our development teams need to work very cooperatively, sometimes having to wait for others to complete changes before making their own.*

3. *Careful consideration must be given to a shared piece of code so as not to harm the intended effects it has on other parts of the system, making development more complex.*

4. *Dependent code must be tracked carefully and kept together in releases so that it does not break when installed at a client site.*

Those are just some examples of the *costs.* The One Architecture strategy also has a number of advantages or *benefits:*

1. *Cerner clients have the chance to implement a true system of care on a common platform extending from the living room to the operating room.*

2. *The unified architecture eliminates a costly, complex, benefit-limiting, and fragile process for our clients, one of writing interfaces between disparate solutions. New Cerner solutions become more attractive because they work with existing solutions.*

3. *Information flows freely across an entire community. The diabetic person's glucose taken at home becomes a part of both his or her personal health record as well as the physician's medical record.*

4. *Clinical and demographic data can be aggregated and studied, making every clinical event a learning event, yielding new clinical and operational insights and knowledge.*

At the time we decided on the One Architecture strategy, the industry pundits said that it couldn't be done. We modeled the likely future with what we knew about our strengths—intelligence, ingenuity, perseverance, strong systems thinking, and a certain amount of audacity—and we decided it was worth the risk. Hiring very smart, personable people and creating the work environment for them to solve complex problems together became practices that supported our strategy. One Architecture has been a very successful strategy that has created a significant competitive advantage.

Strategy is a clever way of achieving an objective. Strategy is also very durable and typically becomes a part of the fabric of how a company thinks and operates. It takes both clever, creative strategies and skillful tactics to achieve a mission. The military engineer's tactical detail of creating a fuel supply line might seem less important than the general's mobile heavy armament strategy, but if the tank division runs out of fuel, the entire mission is in peril.

Strategy is very easy to copy. Copying strategy is itself a very common business *tactic* (for example, all of Domino's Pizza's competitors now deliver). That is why over time, there is little sustainable competitive advantage in business, resulting in few so-called "natural" monopolies. (A natural monopoly is one in which a single supplier proves to be more efficient in the long run than multiple, competitive ones.) We feel the effects of copied strategy in our business. After Y2K, I was very clear within Cerner that we had only a couple of years before all of our competitors would be touting their versions of *HNA Millennium* in the marketplace, basically claiming that they can do it better than Cerner. In the last half of 2002, this prediction became a reality. Eclipsys was heralding *XA*, IDX was heralding *CareCast*, GE was heralding *Centricity*, Siemens was heralding *Soarian*: all were shooting directly at our backs. In a competitive market, it is clear to all competitors what works. Sooner or later, all will copy what works.

While strategy is easy to copy, the plagiarist usually is not quickly successful in the strategy. This is because cultures are powerful. One of my favorite sayings is, "Culture eats strategy for lunch, every day." A key to success is to make your core strategies a part of your culture, creating long-term, durable strategies.

Figure 4.6 illustrates that successful strategies stay in place for a very long time. In it, you also can see a slow evolution of strategy over time.

Check out the old favorite Cerner slide in Figure 4.7. In it, we use the Microsoft Office suite to illustrate that Cerner is not the only company that believes that a common, interoperable architecture is a good strategy.

It amazes me how long it takes to learn whether some of our key strategies are correct. For example, during the first half of the 1990s, when HBOC

Core Business Strategies

Core Business Strategy	Description & History	Business Impact	Tactical Implementation	Comments
Mission-Critical Systems	Was one of the core strategies for Cerner; articulated in 1981; strategy was to invest first in applications that supported the industry's mission —addressing people's medical problems—because it created more value.	Positioned Cerner as the "clinical" company in the market; it took decades but it became a big deal after Y2K.	This drove the sequence of development; clinical first:—Laboratory, Radiology, Pharmacy, Hospital, Physician Office, and so on. Management and Account for Care were late in the sequence.	By not competing against the financial systems, we avoided head-to-head competition with the largest players in the first decade.
Person-Centric Architecture	Was one of the shifts from the 1980s to the 1990s; first articulated around 1992; Millennium is designed around the "person".	Now that entire countries are specifying HCIT, it is essential.	Data model must define Person at its root structure; relationships defined to multiple providers.	This is the foundation for a Personal Health Record.
One Architecture	We have always believed that there will be a layer created in our communities that will be used to coordinate care across our fragmented healthcare system. This will require for some period of time, a common architecture.	All of our solutions are created against a common data model, technical architecture, application architecture, and reusable application code sets	Each development team is required to comply with a common set of standards and use reusable code. Time pressures, client demands, and interlocking priorities makes compliance difficult.	This drives huge positive economics for Cerner; also creates a level of technical complexity and management difficulty.
Grow Organically	Cerner grows through a core competency of developing Intellectual Property and leveraging past investments in HNA by innovating and investing in the development of new solutions and entering new markets. This strategy dates back to our beginning in September 1979.	We invest more of our revenues in IP development (architecture, software and knowledge content).	We will invest more than $1 B over the next five years in new IP development.	Huge impact on our cash flow; shareholders are always nervous about the magnitude of the investment.

Figure 4.6 – Core Business Strategies

(now McKesson) was consolidating the industry by buying everything in sight, most Wall Street analysts thought our expensive, development-centric strategy was wrong. Now, everyone is scrambling to be or sound like Cerner. Strategies are vital to *i*T.

A Compelling Fact: "Architecture Matters"

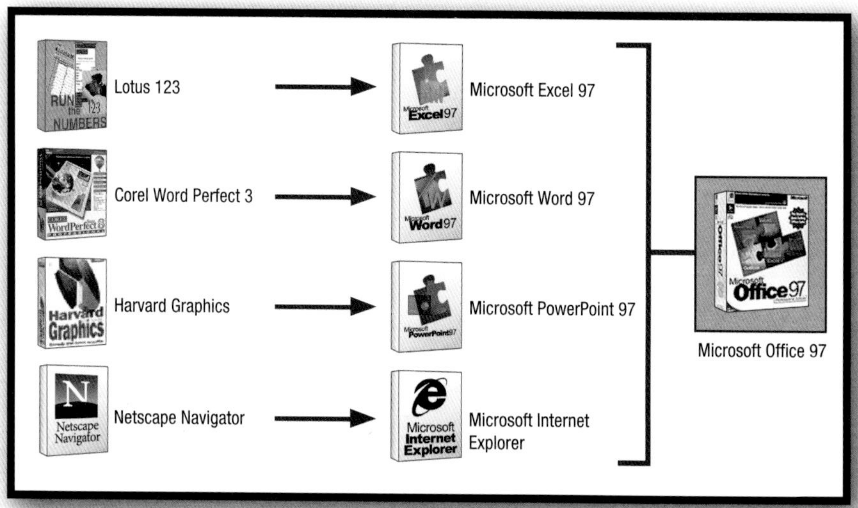

Figure 4.7 – Architecture Slide, circa 1998

Structure: Organizing the Enterprise

Structure is the way you choose to arrange the relationship of people and functions within an enterprise. Structure follows strategy, please! Inexperienced managers will almost always plan structure before strategy because structure is not as abstract as strategy. It is easy to draw org charts, but no manager can rightly know how to structure capabilities and resources until he or she defines the core business strategies.

The nature of an organization is linear—who reports to whom, and how various business functions are organized. How we are organized is a management decision. It must be made very carefully, with an effort to envision *the outcome*.

I believe three principles should guide any manager making decisions about how to structure an organization:

- *Clarity: All associates should be clear as to what is expected of them in their roles, how decisions are to be made, and to whom they report.*

- *Alignment: Every team and business unit in the organization should be aligned with others so that all of the energy, resources, and expenditures are working toward a common mission and are not in conflict.*

- *Focus: Given clarity and team alignment, each associate is in an environment that enables focusing on getting his or her part of the mission accomplished.*

Clarity, alignment, and focus are guidelines. You should consider all three when designing an organizational structure, but you will not be able to optimize all three for everyone in the organization. Optimization means creating the perfect or most favorable conditions for something to flourish. Given natural laws and the reality of finite resources, creating the perfect condition for one thing to flourish most certainly means creating less-than-perfect conditions for other objectives. You can optimize only one thing at a time. In the case of 2003's Cerner-in-Cerner (CinC) structure change for the U.S. client organization, we were seeking to optimize our relationship with our clients. We moved from a Line of Business (LOB) model to a client-centric model. Both have served us well, they were each needed at different stages of our growth and in the maturing of underlying business models such as consulting, sales, and client management.

Organizational Design Considerations

Here are some additional things I think you should consider when designing organizations.

Depth of the Organization

Bureaucracy thrives in layers. Each management tier in the organization represents a layer that moves our clients and associates further away from the chief executive. Try to have as few layers of management as possible. Stretch your experienced managers and your management superstars with broader spans of control to minimize the layers between the top of the organization and the clients and other real work being done. For most of my Cerner career, my direct reports exceed a dozen in order to minimize the number of management layers and keep me closer to the clients and the development of our intellectual property.

Span of Control

The ultimate determinant of how many layers exist in an organization is the span of control of each manager in the organization. There are a number of variables that need to be considered when deciding how many associates can work for one manager, but I have always believed that fewer than four associates reporting to a manager is not enough and too expensive, but more than seven is probably too many. Special circumstances sometimes dictate that the number of reporting relationships exceeds seven. When this is the case, the reporting managers and associates must be very experienced and expected to operate in a very interdependent fashion.

Natural Centers

Figure out what is most important to the performance of the organization at a given point in time, and try to use it as the axis around which you design the organization and teams. At Cerner, there are a number of reasonable choices:

- *Client business functions, such as sales, consulting, or service*

- *IP development business functions, such as design, development, documentation, testing, or delivery*

- *Managed Services, by client or function*

- *Geography, such as country, state, or ZIP code*

- *Type of client, such as large, medium, or small*

- *Markets, such as hospitals, physician offices, labs, or radiology*

- *Market segments, such as Academic Hospitals, Children's Hospitals, Community Hospitals, and IDNs.*

The natural tendency is for managers to optimize their organizations around their own needs to best perform their responsibilities. It's hard to argue with that logic, right? Organizing around your own needs, however, is exactly what you do not want to have happen. Cerner is not trying to optimize the performance of the individual units of organization. All organizational designs must be tested with the "eye of the client," considering what is the best organization for Cerner to serve our clients' wants and needs.

NEAL PATTERSON

Build Accountability Into the New Organization

Accountability must be built into the design of our organization. While organizational changes will bedevil our internal reporting systems, these systems must be changed to accommodate a timely system of measuring and reporting about the performance of each unit of the new organization. The tendency is to compromise and change the organization without changing our internal reporting systems. Resist the tendency. Do the work.

Projects Versus Processes

Projects (Engagements) have starts and finishes. Processes are continuous. Do not confuse the two. They must be organized and managed very differently.

Teams

We all understand how rewarding it is to be a part of a team. Teams often have more capability than the sum contributions of individual performers and therefore are able to take on much bigger missions, resulting in more exciting achievements. When possible, create structure in such a way that people have the chance to participate in team life.

Design Decision-Making Into Structure and Process

The need to deliver business results necessitates that organizations make timely and quality decisions. When you design structure and process, make sure that you are very clear how decisions will be made inside an organization. In a purely hierarchical organizational structure, it is easy to identify what doorstep to darken when a decision needs to be made or a dispute resolved. As you approach the top of a large, complex knowledge organization, however, it can be difficult for any one executive or manager to have the perspective needed to make decisions that affect large segments of your business or large groups of people.

In cases when the concept of a single decision-maker is not practical, I use the technique of interlocking cabinets as a major quasi-structural method for ensuring quick decision-making throughout an organization. A cabinet is just a group of lead executives or managers for a particular area of the company who meet on a predefined interval to make decisions. Cerner's Executive Cabinet is made up of the top company officers at the corporate level. For our meetings, we create a best-guess structured agenda in advance, with each member freely placing topics onto the pre-agenda, but we also begin each meeting by interactively compiling the final agenda and prioritizing the topics. We meet until all of the agenda items have been worked through. When we make a decision, we attach a name to that decision to ensure follow-through. I use the term "live bullets" to convey that the decisions we make during our meetings are *final and effective immediately*. We have a culture of timely decision making.

All Executive Cabinet members are expected to attend, and on the rare occasion when they are unable to attend, they send their next-in-charge executive as their proxy. I am not responsible for briefing anyone who misses a meeting. I started this method when Cerner exceeded $100 million in revenues and 300 associates. It still works as we near $1 billion in revenues and exceed 6,000 associates working all over the world.

The interlocking part of the concept refers to using some of the same members of the Executive Cabinet to seed cabinets at the next level of the organization. Today at Cerner, we have a CinC President Cabinet, a

Functional-Operations Cabinet, and an Architecture Cabinet. At least one member of Cerner's Executive Cabinet participates in each of the other cabinets. Having the cabinets interlock aids the flow of information and makes quick decision-making possible. Another interlocking technique we use is to have joint cabinet sessions on a set, periodic basis. Again, consistent interaction and communication are the keys to creating clarity around how, why, and when decisions are made, and who makes them.

Matrix Organizations

A matrix organization is one in which a person has multiple reporting relationships. The name "matrix" comes from the grid-like diagram that is sometimes used to represent the complex relationship of functional organizations (columns) and solution or project organizations (rows). The person in the intersection of a row *and* column reports to both the head of the column and the head of the row. I have a strong dislike for matrix organizations because they produce a lack of clarity around how decisions are made. But in reality, *all knowledge organizations have elements of a matrix in which conflicting goals originate from different parts of an organization.* In theory, a matrix structure is supposed to break down silos; but it accomplishes this goal by putting the least empowered associates in the cross-current of two powerful sets of priorities. Conflicts arise, and the associate must broker the decision, often to the displeasure of one manager. As the old proverb goes, *"No servant can serve two masters. Either he will hate the one and love the other, or he will be devoted to the one and despise the other."* In a war, you would never ask a soldier to report to two commanders. Instead of matrix organizations, I prefer to use the interlocking cabinets structure because the parts that interlock meet face to face and are appropriately empowered to make decisions.

Transference of Knowledge

Knowledge is the lifeblood of an organization like Cerner, especially the tacit, situational knowledge that is found inside an organization as associates perform their roles, dealing with clients and technology. Dispersing knowledge throughout a complex organization is essential, and must be designed into the organization's structure. You must design positions into your organization to make knowledge explicit through formal documentation, knowledge repositories, formal manuals, help systems, and educational events. As a manager, however, you must understand that an enormous amount of knowledge will exist tacitly in the organization. In a knowledge organization, the knowledge, or Intellectual Capital, is at the bottom of the organization where the work is getting done. That is why we all have our personal lists of experts we go to whenever certain issues or problems arise. As companies grow, two things tend to happen that make the movement of knowledge much more difficult. As associates increase in number, the gap between each associate and the field of experts that span the organization increases tremendously. The silos grow taller and deeper. The second thing that happens to larger, especially global, companies is that people within the organization become geographically dispersed. In addition to organizational silos, distance and time zones are added. Each factor compounds the knowledge transfer challenge. You cannot solve this challenge through structure alone. Cerner benefits if you create an atmosphere where learning and teaching are permitted, encouraged, and rewarded. Most investments of time in knowledge transfer pay for themselves very quickly.

Pathology of Organizations

In my opinion, it is impossible to design the perfect organization, and even the best organizational designs are not permanent. Changes in the environment, shifting enterprise priorities, new business strategies, new technologies, new markets, a new geography, loss of key managers, a new aggressive competitor—a whole host of reasons can trigger the need to redesign your organization. It doesn't sound right, but organizations also wear out and become dysfunctional. As organizations mature, the silo effect takes over, and the managers of the different business units start to optimize the results of their own parts at the expense of the whole. I do not know all of the psychology involved, but you cannot let this happen.

As a manager, you will ultimately have reasons to change your organization. Just keep in mind that people fear change, and changing structure will be extremely disruptive. So proceed—but do so with caution. Despite your best planning, you will never be able to anticipate all of the effects of changing structure. If you need to make big changes, make sure that you do it during a time when you will be around to help assess how your organization is assimilating the change. You may need to make some quick adjustments. In other words, do not make major organizational changes and then go on vacation.

Processes: The Moving Parts of the Enterprise

In many ways, success is all about processes. Dr. W. Edwards Deming was clear about that. Deming, widely recognized as the father of the quality movement, believed that if you continuously improve your processes, using measurements to understand and drive those improvements, you win. I absolutely believe that this approach is how you improve quality. Quality alone, however, does not make for a successful enterprise. Deming would certainly disagree with this statement. I suspect he would argue that I am not defining *process* broadly enough. In my way of thinking, Deming often gives the word *process* the meaning that I associate with the word *system*.

At Cerner, processes are the defined, repeatable methods we use to accomplish our work inside an enterprise in a predictable way, for example, the way we prepare a sales proposal or the way we handle a service request. Processes should be directed by our vision, mission, and strategy. They are executed throughout our organizational structure. They are supported by policies and systems. Processes are systematic connections that produce repeatable, predictable results.

As a manager you must be aware that processes become dysfunctional as the organization changes. Growth almost always obsoletes an organization's processes. Keep your head up and assume that there is a radical redesign of process in your future.

Tools: Levers in the Enterprise

Tools are constructed (not naturally occurring) aids in achieving results. Tools are devices we use to make our work easier or our efforts more effective. Processes and tools are closely linked, with the tools often designed as the tangible interface into a process. Tools are powerful, but they also carry a great risk of overuse, under-use, and misuse.

What is it with our human fascination with tools? I cannot tell you the number of times I have seen managers get mesmerized or obsessed over the tools when they need to look up at the more important elements of vision, mission, and strategy. At Cerner, tools can include the hardware devices we use, such as laptop computers and mobile phones, but more often they are software applications, applets, and macros that support processes and administrative tasks such as daily communication, annual performance evaluations, time and expense accounting, client intelligence gathering, and service request tracking. On the IP side of our organization, quite an extensive tool set has been used for the enforcement of functional and engineering methodologies, configuration management, automated testing, and defect tracking. Tools also can include the programming languages and platforms that support our development strategies. Our Client organization has accumulated a large number of tools to assist in the implementation and support of our applications in our clients' environments.

Have you ever heard the expression, "If you have a hammer, everything looks like a nail"? Managers, be wary of using a hammer just because you have it. When tools are detached from correct vision, mission, strategy, structure, or process, they can be very misleading and dangerous things. Also, be careful with expensive or obsolete tools. If you invest a lot of time or money into purchasing or developing a tool, then you are going to have a pretty hefty bias toward using it, whether it is right or not. I have watched Cerner managers fail to see the future because of their past investment in tools. The old-timers will remember MASS-11, WordPerfect, Lotus 1-2-3, and Harvard Graphics. There will be times in your management career when the best thing you can do for your team is to walk away from a tool. This can be costly, both in terms of morale and the need to purchase or redesign another tool set. Your best bet is to choose tools carefully, and make sure they support what you are trying to accomplish. To do that, you have to have your vision, mission, strategy, structure, and process aligned.

Effort vs. Results

"I'm not really in the excuse business. We have this expression, 'Don't tell me about the pain, show me the baby.'" – Bill Parcells on 60 Minutes, Oct. 3, 2004

Did you notice that effort is not represented in the graphic of the V^2 algorithm? In or around 1990, I created a big internal debate over a companywide screen saver that said *Cerner Values Results, Not Effort.* Many years later, I created an even bigger debate through an e-mail that seriously challenged the amount of effort we were putting toward our vision.

So what is the truth in these seemingly opposing messages? Do I value effort, or don't I? The truth is I don't *and* I do.

I *don't* value effort, because, as adult human beings and as a company, none of us can afford to value effort over results. It struck me, with the internal debate over the screen saver, that a few Cerner associates perhaps were relating professional outcomes to the outcomes of their kids' soccer teams. In the case of the soccer game, it is completely appropriate to value effort over accomplishments. The point that seemed to be lost on that contingent was that, at Cerner, we are *not* kids still growing and exploring our skills, but professionals being paid to produce results. Try telling Lamar Hunt, the owner of the Kansas City Chiefs, that the team's defense is trying hard, but cannot produce wins. See how well that argument goes. Results, not effort, are what our clients expect, demand, and value. Results must be valued on a corporate level, on a team level, and on an individual level. The day that we can afford to value effort over results is the beginning of the end.

I *do* value effort because, as a human being, I place a tremendous value on time, both my own and that of others. Because of our intrinsic mortality, I consider time to be the most precious resource any of us can give one another. I get that time spent doing one thing means time not spent doing another. Whereas results speak to my brain, effort hits me at the heart level. I was as touched by the incredible effort expended by the

Cerner U.K. team in 2003 as I was troubled by the lack of effort demonstrated by a limited number of associates in 2001, well documented in my infamous e-mail message. Your time and effort toward a given goal speak a great deal of the value you place on it.

In the scope of companies (potential employers) and visions out there, Cerner has one of the more profound visions. Because we are working in healthcare, affecting people's lives, the demands are always going to require a big effort. If you ask me whether *you* should give your time, hard work, and effort to Cerner, I say—with no sarcasm whatsoever—that only *you* can decide if it is worth it for *you*. If our work isn't meaningful to you, then any amount of effort will seem like too much.

Ideally, effort is the energy we expend once the vision, mission, strategy, structure, process, and tools are in place. The discussion of results comes sequentially at the end of the V^2 algorithm, because the other variables must be there *and aligned* for the effort not to be wasted. This is what it really means to work smarter and not just harder.

Results (A, T, V): Value for Clients, Shareholders, & Associates

When you combine all of the elements in the algorithm—vision, mission, strategy, structure, processes, tools, and effort—results are what are produced. At Cerner, a result is an outcome that creates value for clients, shareholders, or associates. Business results are never accidental. *Your primary role as a manager is to control the factors needed to deliver business results against a plan.*

At Cerner we seek a number of results. Here are some examples of outcomes that help us measure success:

- *Corporate financial outcomes: Revenue growth, EPS growth, return on equity, DSOs, cash collections, operating margin, operating earnings, stock price*

- *Market share outcomes: corporate bookings, contract signings, win-loss ratios, displacements of major competitors*

- *Consulting engagement outcomes: client business results, satisfied clients, contract profitability, engagement profitability, on-time conversions, physicians using CPOE, contract extensions*

- *Client service outcomes: client loyalty, client satisfaction, add-on sales, client profitability*

- *IP development outcomes: on-time delivery, client satisfaction, market share of solution, profitability of solution, software reuse, third-party license costs, patents awarded, articles published, papers presented, speaking engagements, research grants awarded*

- *Associate outcomes: associate satisfaction, associate retention, number of new leaders (promotions)*

Results must be measured, as there can be no management without measurement. The value of results must be inherent in the measurement. One key attribute of value in this management sense is a client's willingness to pay an amount greater than our total cost to create and deliver the solution or service. The difference between our total cost and the client's total revenues is our inherent operating profitability.

Results have three attributes:

A – *Attainment*

T – *Trend*

V – *Variance*

As a manager, you will learn to look very closely at results and these three attributes that measure them.

A – *Managers Attain Goals and Objectives*

Attainment refers to the realization of a goal or objective, the achievement of a discrete, measurable result. The attained result, which is to be compared to the planned result, could be releasing software on time and under the planned cost, meeting a quarterly sales goal, accomplishing a major conversion on time and under the planned cost, or earning a high client satisfaction rating; the list of potential discrete results is great. Your success or failure in attaining a specific result is frequently the *only* measurement an outsider will see of your management capability. Too many failures and your management career is over. This thought is captured in the saying, "You are smarter when you make your numbers." I like to joke that, as CEO, my IQ is clearly a function of the stock price. Attainment of a specific result doesn't guarantee a manager's success, but it is a very good start. It is very hard to succeed in business without a strong history of consistently delivering results.

T – *Managers Manage Trends*

Trend is the sine and slope over time. What do you think is more valuable to a business: a long-term pattern of one or two quarters of great results far exceeding plan, followed by several quarters of below-plan, poor results; or results that are consistently at or above the operating plan, with each quarter higher than the previous? No contest. The latter is much more valuable because of the meeting or exceeding of the plan AND the positive trend, indicative of growth. It is not so much the actual attainment but the trend of attainment over time and the rate of improvement (or decrease) that define a venture's success (or failure). There is nothing more satisfying to a manager than continuously improving performance (rising sine and slope). Conversely, there is nothing more stressful than deteriorating performance (falling sine and slope). As they say in medicine, all bleeding ultimately will stop. In both business and biology, if the trend is negative long enough, you flat-line. One of the most important things you manage is the trend.

V – Managers Manage Variance (Quality)

Variance is a statistic that describes the amount of spread in the distribution or, in other words, the ability for results to be consistent. It is a measurement of quality. A high degree of variance around the trend line is a clear indicator of a quality problem. Even with a positive trend, a high degree of variance will create a "saw blade" trend line and a very unsteady ride. Variance is also the difference between the planned result and the actual result. If an organization experiences a high level of variance, then the organization cannot produce repeatable or planned results. It is very difficult to operate in this mode for any extended period of time. In business, absent any clearer explanation of the problem, this is typically indicative of a quality problem with the process or skills of the people. As a manager, you are responsible for measuring and developing processes and skills that minimize the variance from plan. The good manager finds the root causes of the variance and makes immediate changes. Overachievement is a positive form of variance, but in many cases it still indicates a quality problem with the plan. Our results should exceed our clients' expectations, but they should seldom exceed our own.

****

Time and again, I have used the Vision-to-Value algorithm as a technique for self-examination, and as a method of solving major problems for others. When one of Cerner's teams or endeavors is having a problem, the V^2 algorithm proves invaluable for deeper inspection.

As a manager, you are always measuring and studying the trends and variances of your organization's results. If the results are not there, something is wrong. Results are like traffic signals for managers. If they are green, indicated by positive attainment, trend, and variance, you may go forward (always looking both ways for hazards in your environment). If results are red, indicated by a clear-cut lack of attainment, you as a manager must stop and find the flaws in the plan. If they are yellow (positive attainment but unsuccessful trends or too much variance over time), you must cautiously inspect the plan and look for ways to improve it. Yellow-light results are the hardest to deal with. Your temptation will be to just try to go faster to beat the light. This is a mistake.

When I see missed results, poor trends, or too much variance over time, I collect and examine data on each attribute in a top-down, bottom-up inspection. (See Chapter 7, "From Sand to Gems", for a more complete discussion of top-down, bottom-up thinking.) I start at the top of the V^2 algorithm and ask if the manager has a genuine, compelling vision and one that fits with Cerner's vision. If the manager has a solid vision, then I continue my examination of each lower element. Once I understand the picture from the top down, I begin to verify what it really looks like at the bottom. This is the bottom-up part of the inspection. The trick is to start from the top so you won't be overwhelmed or misled by the issues you see at the bottom. People around you will want you to go straight to the perceived source of the issue—typically something in the middle, a broken process or tool. Usually this is just a symptom. Until you find the top-most source of the problem, I guarantee you that it *will* repeat. When problems repeat, you are failing as a manager.

It really amazes me how easy it is to find the flaws in an enterprise by using the V^2 algorithm and following its implied sequence. Develop a discipline that when you do not like the results your organization is producing, you rethink the entire formula, working top-down, bottom-up. If you have enough facts, you will find the flaws in your plan.

V^3 Calculus: Factoring Velocity Into Vision-to-Value

"Even if you're on the right track, you'll get run over if you just sit there."
- Mark Twain

The Vision-to-Value algorithm described in this chapter has helped me bring many solutions to market and ideas to reality. After using the algorithm many times, however, I can say with confidence that merely executing the algorithm is not enough to guarantee success. To do that, you must manage one additional variable, a vector that runs through the entire algorithm: *velocity*.

Physics students will tell you that velocity is a vector comprised of direction and speed. Correct velocity is imperative to creating value. In business, time is your enemy. Time adds to your cost. Time gives your competitors an opportunity to beat you in the market. My experience is that, in business, if you wait long enough…something bad will happen. Too much speed, though, or even a slightly wrong direction, and you will lose your control. Your results will suffer. As a manager, you need to actively manage your velocity, both direction and speed, as you move through the elements in the algorithm.

****

To conclude, the algorithm I have described in this chapter is the way to get from vision, the place where all of our ideas start, to value, the moment when we deliver results to our clients that exceed their expectations. There is nothing I can impart to you that is more quintessentially "Cerner" than a means for driving an idea from vision to value.

CHAPTER FOUR

Chapter Five

Managing People—
Our Greatest Assets

The creation of a thousand forests is in one acorn.
– Ralph Waldo Emerson

This chapter and the next are going to delve into the objects of management—the people and things being managed. I devote a whole chapter to the management of people, because *they are by far the most important and complex management responsibility you will ever have.*

Although producing business results against a plan is your primary role as a manager, the task of effectively managing the associates who report to you will always be the key to any high performance organization. If the system is working correctly, you will even be held accountable for this important responsibility.

Over the years, I have gone through a personal evolution on this subject. In my career before Cerner, I gained a lot of experience in leading teams—project teams. Frankly, I was very good at it. My projects were on time and on budget, and my clients valued the results. Growing and running a company, however, turned out to differ significantly from leading a project. The dynamic inside a project is such that you know every team member and can assess their strengths and weaknesses. They also know you as a leader. That in essence makes you a team. Projects have starts and finishes, and they typically have clear goals and objectives. Projects are very much like playing a football game. You work hard to get the best team possible, but on game day you line up the players you have, get highly motivated to beat the other team, and put all of your energy and focus on winning. Organizations, if things go well, exist in perpetuity and have visions and missions, along with many other measures of qualitative, operational, and financial performance. The manager who can keep a team of people highly motivated and who can direct them well over long periods of time is a true artist—and has my respect.

I remember passing two noteworthy milestones caused by growth that forced me to think more about the role of Cerner managers in guiding Cerner associates. The first milestone was the day I realized that I did not know everyone working at Cerner. Because of Cerner's history as an entrepreneurial company, I have vivid memories of the era when I knew *every* associate, and many times also their spouses, children, and even parents. That situation slowly changed until there came a day when I realized that I no longer knew every associate, and from that point forward, I never would again. I have lost track of the date, but I am sure that it was in the mid 1980s. The second milestone was the day I realized that not everyone at Cerner knew who I was. That date was in the late 1980s. I was giving a Cerner tour to one of the National Health Service Chief Scientific Officers for Northwest Thames in England, Dr. Harold Glass. As I took him into the data center in the 2800 building, an associate stopped me, wanted to know what I was doing, and informed me that I was not authorized to be there.

Dr. Glass laughed. He seemed to understand quite clearly what had just happened. I pondered the significance of knowing that not everyone knew me. My reach had hit its limits. Cerner's future was no longer a function of the entrepreneur. I knew for certain that day that only

Cerner's managers could determine how motivated and directed our organization would be in the future.

My Assumptions in Thinking About Associates

Assumption #1: It Takes an Army

The first thing that needs to be established is that accomplishing anything of significance takes more effort than any one person can give. I have clearly reclusive tendencies and really prefer to work without the interdependency of cooperating and coordinating with others. Jeanne Patterson (I am her husband) calls my home office *Neal's cave*. She knows that I go into the cave to be alone, to focus, and to concentrate. A lot of my ideas come from the solitude of my cave. Ideas are cheap, though, and have virtually no value. Converting ideas into a reality takes an army, and an army needs a great deal of organization and management. To accomplish the Cerner vision and mission, it takes an army of us, each with clarity of purpose, near-perfect alignment with one another, and the ability to focus on getting our own jobs done.

Assumption #2: The Army Is All-Volunteer

In our army, there is no conscription or draft. In ours, everyone is a volunteer, one day at a time. No employment contracts bind the individuals on our teams to Cerner. To be sure, almost everyone has a mortgage or car payment that motivates them to come to work, but the reality is that every person at Cerner can find work elsewhere. All we can do to keep our associates at Cerner is to create a compelling environment that challenges, grows, and rewards the individual. If you are a team leader or front-line manager, you have the primary responsibility for creating this environment. Everyone in a management position, however, shares the responsibility and challenge of creating a highly motivated workforce. Think about how you can make that happen. Now you should understand why I consider the *Command and Control* and *Abusive* styles of management (see Chapter 1) to be inconsistent with our company's culture.

Assumption #3: Fear Is Present

There is an interesting relationship between emotions of trust and fear. You trust someone whose behavior you can comfortably predict in a broad range of circumstances. You fear someone whose behavior you cannot comfortably predict AND who can do harm to you, your loved ones, or something else you value. As a manager, you hold a degree of power over the associates in your organization. You have influence over their advancement, their compensation, and even their continued employment. This puts you in the category of people who can do harm to their careers and impact their families.

It is very easy to forget this. You probably do not spend a lot of time thinking about the power you wield over the people who work side by side with you every day, and people will not usually show their fear to you directly. When dealing with associates who report to you, however, you must *assume* that an element of fear is always present in your relationship. That is why I have written a great deal about the need to be trustworthy and consistent when dealing with the associates in your organization. These characteristics become the foundation of a trusting and trusted relationship.

As humans, I believe that fear is part of nature's way of conditioning us to survive. Children fear the dark and the monster under the bed. As we grow older, our fears change, but they are still present. Many capable and successful adults fear failure, and that is not necessarily a bad thing. In my career, fear of failure has been my greatest motivator. It has been much more motivating than any reward system, my strong competitive nature to win, or even my desire to succeed. While success can be defined in many ways, failure has a much sharper definition.

Fear arises when we encounter things that are outside of our control. In business there are many things that are outside of our control. *You* are one of the many things that are outside the control of the associates on your team. Because of the nature of your influence over their professional lives, and their normal fear of failure, the associates on your team will manufacture more than enough fears for themselves. You should never use fear to manage.

Although managing by fear may create a temporary appearance of order, it does not work in the long term. Fear creates an organizational culture where innovation is stifled and strong performers leave. Associates will not openly discuss what they think, which will suppress the dialog needed to address complex problems. In the worst cases, it creates situations where unethical behavior is overlooked for fear of retribution. Unaddressed, this type of problem has the potential to destroy a team or company.

Create an open, collaborative environment where healthy disagreements are accepted. Acknowledge and appreciate the high-quality input you receive from members of your team, especially when you ultimately choose to go down a different path. Strive to keep lines of communication open so that associates feel bold enough to share good ideas in the future.

NEAL PATTERSON

Assumption #4: Communication Is Essential

One of the worst things you can do to a human being is to fail to communicate. It breeds fear and irrational behavior. We all remember that dreadful day, September 11, 2001. It was a Tuesday, and at Cerner, we were on the second day of our annual client conference, the Cerner Health Conference, in Kansas City. It was our biggest day of the conference. The keynote speaker was Matt Ridley, a British author who had recently published the book *Genome*. Matt was scheduled to deliver the keynote speech to our group of nearly 3,000 guests and probably nearly another 1,000 Cerner associates at 9:30 A.M. Prior to that, at around 8:00 A.M., I and several others were with Matt when we learned about the towers at the World Trade Center. As we watched news coverage, it became clear that the United States was under terrorist attack, and many thoughts were going through our heads. We were on the clock, however, and had to make decisions, including whether to cancel or keep his talk. It was unanimous in the room; we did not want the terrorists to change what we had planned. To do so would seem to give them a victory.

Immediately, we knew that all of our out-of-town guests would want to go home, and we were just beginning to learn that the nation's airline system was shut down, with no idea as to when it would return. As we entered the convention hall where Matt was to speak, two huge screens intended for the speaker's presentation were showing live feeds and news analysis on CNN. In a surreal environment, we started the session with a moment of silence. Then we announced the creation of a provisional communication center and relayed our just-formed conference and logistics strategy to the audience. It was time for Matt to speak. That's when someone turned off the CNN feed. I jumped out of my seat and ran backstage to the control center. A manager had decided beforehand that we wanted people to focus on Matt

Ridley; after all we had flown him from England to make the presentation. I completely understood the logic of shutting off the news feed, but I disagreed strongly with the result. I approached Matt and said to him, "This will be your decision, but in my opinion, one of the worst things you can do to a human is to create uncertainty."

The show went on. Matt's slides on one screen described how we as a human race have discovered, using our intellect, how all living things are created, while images on the second screen showed how we as a human race are trying, through hate, to destroy a major portion of ourselves. We all watched both screens. Matt was brilliant.

In the hours and then days that followed, Cerner as an organization performed impeccably in managing the crisis, demonstrating our skills as managers and our compassion as human beings. With the nation's airlines grounded, we arranged transportation home for our clients by charter buses, limos, and cars. As we began, along with the rest of the world, to deal with the shock and grief caused by that day, communication remained essential.

Styles of Communication

In communication, style is important. *Transactional Analysis* is a popular branch of psychology that provides a useful model for understanding communication between two people. One of the theories of Transactional Analysis is that the state of mind you display in your initial communication will likely dictate (but not necessarily match) the state of mind offered to you in response. If you start communicating with someone on your team in parent mode, his or her tendency is to become the child. At Cerner, we want adults on our teams, not children. The way to consistently achieve this is to grow the habit of dealing with people in an adult-to-adult mode. Too many managers insist on taking the role of parent in their transactions, almost assuredly forcing the associates who report to them into the role of child. This does not achieve the results we want in a business setting, and it is unacceptable given that it is so easy to do differently. If you have a young child or are around one, run the experiment. Start an adult conversation with him or her. You will soon see a five-year-old in the adult mode. Think.

I believe we all develop a variety of methods of interacting with one another. With regard to communication, I have never held myself out as someone to model. Conventional forms of communication have never been easy for me. Growing up in relative isolation on a farm, I developed my own language as a child. At the age of five, the only person who could understand me was my older brother. Even my *mother* had to ask Kent to interpret. To make matters worse, and as I often relate, I started school one year early so that Joe McCray would have a playmate—true story. It wasn't long before I was making a 100-mile round trip to Enid, Oklahoma, much of it on dirt roads, to see the speech pathologist to be taught how to speak. Recently, I have found out that learning to speak is driven by a set of genes that actually turn off after a certain age. That is why young kids instinctively learn languages—not just their mother tongue, but any to which they are exposed early and often enough. Obviously, more evidence of me being a mutant— my language genes were never on.

Do not use my style of communication. I am almost always speaking adult to adult, but I am too direct for some people. I also have a level of impatience integrated into my transactional style that many people find offensive. I often come across as this highly competitive, driven, entrepreneurial, impatient person on a mission, complete with an attitude.

In the introduction to this chapter, I mentioned that there were two distinct moments when I realized my reach as a manager had its limits.

CHAPTER FIVE

There was a third, much more conspicuous, moment that occurred in April of 2001. Any of you who are reading this book and were here will remember well when I wrote the most widely read e-mail in the history of computing. It was my 15 minutes of…well, infamy. For those of you who were not here, let me create some context. The last half of the 1990s was "the perfect storm" for Cerner, a very difficult period, primarily due to our decision to completely rebuild our technology and architecture with *HNA Millennium*. The trials of that period were compounded by the tremendous added stress during 1998 and 1999 of undertaking literally hundreds of projects that had to be completed successfully before midnight (local time), December 31, 1999—the infamous Y2K. Further, our challenge was made more difficult by the bleak business environment caused for Cerner by the passage of the federal Balanced Budget Act of 1997, which shrunk all of our clients' operating margins. It *was* the perfect storm; there was extreme stress throughout Cerner. The morning of January 1, 2000, was the dawn of a new era. I had both internally and externally predicted in mid-1999 that we were going to have a great start to the new millennium. I foresaw and started saying that this was the decade healthcare would embrace information technology as the answer to many of its systemic issues. I was very confident and excited, but Cerner was very tired and stressed.

I expected and even wanted the tempo to back off for a while in the first half of 2000. It did, but then it never came back. I started discussing this during Cabinet meetings in the summer of 2000. You could feel that the air was out of the balloon. Cerner was not working toward our vision and mission; there was an overall attitude that we had enough vision. There was considerable circumstantial evidence to support this fact, including full-time associates who were putting in *fewer* than 40 hours each week. Associates were coming late to work, and leaving early. It was a small group, of course, but enough that some longtime associates were beginning to express concern to me about the company's disappearing work ethic. Finally, after arriving at the office at 8:00 one morning in 2001 to a sparse parking lot, I sat down and wrote the most famous e-mail in history. I vented my frustration and concern to the Cerner management team. I suspect that I actually wrote it in five to seven minutes. An untold part of the story is that I did actually pause before clicking Send. I sensed that my directness and cynicism were acidic. I called my assistant, Kynda Goodwin, to review it, knowing it was very pointed. We grabbed Marc Naughton, Cerner's CFO, for another perspective. I recall Kynda's response: "This will not bother the managers who are doing their job, but it will be offensive to the managers who have allowed the work ethic to deteriorate." In fact, her reaction sounded like just what I wanted! I searched for whom to send the message to. I scanned the distribution lists (DLs) in Outlook's Global Address List, and I found one that looked promising: DL_ALL_MANAGERS. I clicked Send.

Luckily I didn't use obscenities, but the e-mail did paint a very vivid picture of a Cerner none of us wanted, for the purpose of shocking "ALL MANAGERS" into *doing something* to fix the problem. If *you* were to adopt for a moment my direct, satirical, and sometimes impatient transactional style, and use it to send an electronic message to people, many of whom have no relationship with *you* or context for your communication, *you* would probably not like the results. Trust me.

In this instance, the results were quick in coming. The e-mail was intentionally leaked, causing all sorts of havoc. While the intended context was manager (me) to all Cerner managers, some managers immediately sent it directly to their associates. Others sent it outside the company. Within hours, it was all over the Internet. Our stock price dropped significantly. The

Kansas City Star ran a front-page story on it, directly quoting "investors" who were actually unverifiable sources from unmoderated Internet chat boards. The next week, I made the front page of the *New York Times* business section, and after that, the e-mail was covered in every major paper in the world. It is used in a college course to teach students how *not* to manage and communicate.

Although I can usually take quite a bit of heat without it getting to me, I lost sleep over this incident. Ninety-nine percent of the people painted me a villain. I was called evil, obsolete, incompetent, and a number of words unfit for publication even here.

In the episode I went through with the e-mail, I felt disappointed on many fronts. With myself, for not carefully considering my audience and for allowing fear to become part of my management arsenal. With the managers who lacked judgment and sent it directly to our associates. And with the individuals who posted this e-mail, along with other internal communications, immediately to a variety of Internet chat boards in clear violation of Cerner policy, not to mention any sense of loyalty to our company and its associates. It was really disturbing to realize that there were individuals within Cerner who apparently wanted to bring harm to their own company.

This poignant life experience crystallized some big lessons for me. The first is the extreme importance of a personal relationship with the people who work with you. The DL_ALL_MANAGERS address list was loaded with managers with whom I had no *contextual relationship*. "No relationship" is a breeding ground for mistrust and miscommunication. And once the e-mail was shared with the thousands of Cerner associates, the only real context was the words in the e-mail. The second lesson is that when you have a problem, fix it. Problems never go away until some willing manager does their top-down, bottom-up thinking and fixes it. This incident caused me to back away from the problem that I had so curtly described. We were in the middle of one of the biggest growth periods in the history of the company. My prediction of how well Cerner would do at the start of this decade came true, as well as my other prediction of how completely healthcare would embrace information technology. I had also said, however, that our competitors would all copy our message and strategies. They did just that. Two years later, I dealt with a version of the same problem, a symptom of not having fully fixed the root of the problem. This time I did not write an e-mail. I did what managers do—studied the problem, built a plan, executed the plan, and put controls in place to make sure that my plan was sound and was being followed. One final lesson from this episode: Always *think* before you click Send.

Modes of Communication

One of the major drivers toward the adoption of information technology is its ability to help us connect and communicate. Make the list: faxes, e-mail, instant messaging, two-way pagers, cell phones, Web sites—all are a continuation of our human desire to communicate, both one-to-one, one-to-many, and many-to-many. We are nearing the state of being "always on" and are probably reaching information overload, with interruptions limiting our attention span and awakening the latent attention deficit disorder in all of us. Over the years, here are the techniques that I have come to believe in and constantly use. As a manager, even if you do not consider yourself a consummate communicator, you must develop your own expertise in communicating, or you will fail your organization.

> **Face to Face:** No communication is more important than the face-to-face encounter. There are a number of business contexts

where this happens—the business lunch, internal meetings, client meetings, the coffee pot, the lunch line, or traveling together. All are sources of high-quality time to communicate, set expectations with team members, and provide valuable feedback on status, issues, and performance. As a manager, you need to be a skilled communicator, and you need to be sensitive to the fact that your team will listen closely to what you say and how you say it, all parts of your communication. I learned many years ago that, as CEO, an offhand comment by me can easily be misinterpreted and unintentionally change the priorities and direction of an entire team. As manager, you need to think about what you are saying and the context of the message before you speak, which is not always an easy thing to do. I am preaching the obvious, but it is almost always better to communicate face to face, in a positive tone, which is not always easy to do in tough situations where things are not going well. It is many degrees more important, however, to be positive when things are afoul. You are going to need the entire team's energy and skills to recover. If you are delivering a negative message, be positive, be precise, be timely, give details, describe the consequences, and clearly define an action at the end.

The most important type of face-to-face communication in which you will engage as a manager is the formal Annual Performance Review that you are responsible to conduct with your team members. I like to think about it as an annual interview instead of performance review. Part of the reason is that if there are any performance issues, they should have been addressed as they arose during the year. That way, the annual meeting is truly quality time in which to explore a number of career and business topics with your associate. This is not administration, it is management of the highest order. Yes, there are some administrative duties in connection with the meeting, such as preparing assessments and filling out online forms, but this is not meaningless bureaucracy. The meeting is is your most important moment of the year with your associate. I take this task as a duty to those who work directly for me. Although I am not perfect in all of the details, I have developed an annual process where I block an entire week off to be able to prepare, conduct, and document this important task.

A homework assignment is usually given asking your associate to prepare an Annual Self Appraisal. I review the associate's assessment as well as notes from prior years. If the associate has spent a portion of the review period working for another manager, I consult with the other manager prior to making my evaluation. Then I prepare for the interview by making my own assessment of the associate's successes and failures for the time period under review, as well as the projects that are too early to call. Then I document what I consider to be the individual's strengths, weaknesses, and areas that need to be improved. I think through how to set clear expectations about the associate's future in the company.

Allow adequate time for the actual interview, at least 90 minutes, though I prefer two hours. It is important to do the administrative items first. Give the annual performance evaluation and compensation increase (if known) up front. Not to do so devalues the time you are investing because the associate is anxious to hear these very important details. It also frames all of your other comments, either good or bad.

It is extremely important to get any paperwork finished soon after the interview. Try to allow for time immediately following the session to complete the necessary documentation. Copy the associate on anything going into his or her file.

Town Halls: It was Ewing Kauffman, the founder and then-chairman of Marion Merrill Dow, who gave me the advice, "get everyone into one room and talk." Interestingly, the very early Cerner associates will tell you that we have been doing a version of Town Hall ever since we had more than 20 associates. In the beginning, we would go to Woodside Racquet Club; later we had them in Cliff's Place on the third floor of 2800. There they grew to become the "stand-up" meetings, because there was standing room only in the room. Then we started using the Hyatt Ballroom. After we opened the Associate Center in 1994, we used the gymnasium. Eventually, we outgrew even that and started broadcasting the meeting to other sites on campus. Today, we webcast the event around the globe.

Most managers at Cerner know how these meetings operate. I have always been careful to limit them to around two to three hours, with four major parts: a formal presentation of relevant current topics with broad appeal; recognition of performance of outstanding teams (and individuals); a perspective piece from me; and the most important part, interactive Q&A with Cerner associates. My technique of throwing valuable objects into the audience is my backup plan for soliciting questions from the audience.

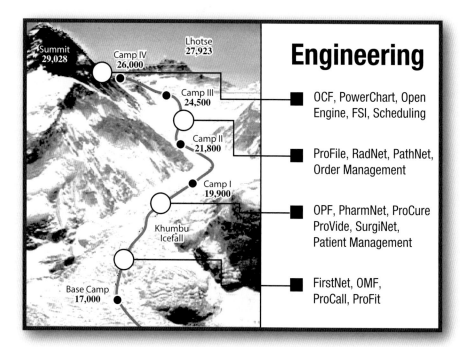

Figure 5.1 – Town Hall Slide, circa 1996

I have a tendency to use metaphors to communicate ideas about Cerner during Town Halls. During the *Cerner Millennium* build and rollout phase of our history, we talked a lot about climbing. At a Town Hall during our perfect storm, we used a picture of mountains and extreme ascents (Figure 5.1) to describe the status of our solutions.

I have been doing Town Halls for more than 20 years—through good times and bad. As a manager, you should get everyone in the same room from time to time. I suggest quarterly or whenever a major issue or event needs to be discussed. I strongly believe that you must always be candid and forthright in these sessions. You will have people all around you wanting to make the event a rah-rah session. There is nothing wrong with including some feel-good content, but know that the associates in your organization are very smart and thoughtful. They will see through almost any attempt to spin a subject. Be honest, be clear, and be open.

Neal Notes: I personally have a love/hate relationship with e-mail. It was during the mid to late 1990s, before our large bet-the-company *Cerner Millennium* architecture stabilized, that I started offering my perspective about a large range of subjects, calling these quickly written e-mails Neal Notes. Externally, some very dynamic changes were occurring. Our industry was shifting during that time, and one of our major competitors, HBOC, was the darling of Wall Street. When McKesson announced in late 1998 that they were going to buy HBOC, a number of pundits claimed that it was over. Game, set, match: they won, we lost. In the same time period, we went through the dot-com era, when the new economy and new technology supposedly made anyone over the age of 30 obsolete. Few associates had the 50,000-foot view of Cerner's prospects and future, so I wrote the notes to help associates keep the faith. Fast-forward to 2003 and the National Health Service (NHS) procurement. I wrote long Neal Notes as we pursued the opportunities in the U.K., and even longer Notes when I found out that we were not going to be awarded the largest of these contracts.

I believe the more things change either internally or externally, the more you as a manager are required to communicate. Associates want perspective, not a PowerPoint on change. You are their manager; they want to know what you think.

NEAL PATTERSON

Let them know. Give the why. Do not depend on the CEO or your manager to communicate with them. You do it. It is called management. That's what managers do.

Social Events: There is a reason that Cerner sponsors social events. It is important for you as the manager to be real and to know more about your associates. There is no better method than through formal and informal social events. You should on occasion have your team to your house, at your expense. I make sure that there is a Patterson Christmas party every year with spouses and children. Jeanne arranges for Santa to come. I have also held relatively large summer parties, just for the sake of being connected and real. The informal events, within commonsense limits, are also a great way to build team spirit.

The goal of these events is not to become intimate friends with the people on your team (a topic addressed in the "Edge" section in Chapter 1). Your goal is to *be a real person* and for you to have a greater understanding of the associates who work for you.

If Cerner is sponsoring a social event and your associates are in attendance, it is mandatory that you be there, preferably with your spouse, children, or significant other. I am sorry, but managing is not an 8-to-5 job.

Personal Projects: As I shared in the introduction, this book is me doing my job as a manager, attempting to extend my reach to more members of the management team. There was no time to do a project like this, and there was certainly no external pressure to complete it. It was, as they say, a labor of love. As a manager, if you think of a project that will help your team, do it. Find the time; make it happen.

Management by Walking Around: I believe in it. Be visible. Be interactive. Be approachable by approaching. Be interested in what your associates are doing. Show it by showing up at their site of work. Be open to their ideas and criticisms. Take every opportunity to be in this mode, for example, when you are riding the elevator or standing in the lunch line. Engage the associate standing next to you and ask, "What are you working on today that will fulfill our vision?" This only works as a management technique if you really listen to the reply.

Communicate Both Ways—Up and Down

I consider communication to be a bidirectional need. I find that the most effective way to communicate *up*, in my case, with Cerner's Board of Directors, is to stop and write a quarterly update, sharing my view of both current events and long-term trends in the industry. I do this usually just prior to meeting with them. In reality, what happens in face-to-face meetings is that, while the expanded bandwidth of person-to-person communication is great, the number of topics you can effectively cover is smaller. In addition to making Board meetings more effective, writing things down also creates a great audit trail of your thinking over time.

I use the annual report letter to do the exact same thing with our shareholders. Although the actual shareholders are dynamic groups of institutions and individuals, I treat them with equal respect by systematically communicating with them my views on our environment, industry, and company. I have resisted making this letter a marketing document. It has my name on it. It should be my thoughts.

NEAL PATTERSON

Even if your boss sits right next to you, make a point of sending a written update now and then. Write a trip report on your way back from a client visit. Send it to both your team and your manager. *Be succinct and relevant* and it will be read. Your manager will appreciate it, and you will be surprised at how the act of putting your thoughts in words clarifies your own actions and direction.

Communicate Clearly: Speak Up

It was Theodore Roosevelt who said, "Speak softly and carry a big stick." We need to define "softly." I have two thoughts on being heard:

First, a meeting is the precise time to speak your opinion. The best way to solve problems is to triangulate them, get multiple views, multiple perspectives. You may have the answer that someone else lacks. Do not be the person who immediately after the meeting has ended starts talking about what you think.

Second, when you speak, project your voice. I believe that if you cannot be heard, then you are not going to be effective. I sit in too many meetings in which someone is not projecting his or her voice loudly enough to be heard. I grew up on tractors with no hearing protection, but I *think* my hearing is adequate. Speak up if you want to be heard, and encourage like behavior in your associates. The meeting room is not the place for tea-time manners.

Assumption #5: Prepare for Disappointment

I have two short sayings to express the fact that, over time, we must be prepared to be disappointed by the actions of people. First, I have often said, *"I do not like computers, but compared to the alternative…."*

And second, I frequently confess, *"My biggest weakness is that I trust people—and I hope I never change."* Your role as a manager is to deal with the paradoxical assumptions behind these two quips. Working with other people is at the heart of what managers do. It will be a source of great joy for you as a manager, but it will also be the hardest part of your job. Humans are by nature emotional and inconsistent. This is normal, and needs to be your presumption going into your job. You must *prepare for disappointment.*

We all have a number of things constantly going on in our lives that add to our occasional unexpected behavior and decisions. The list of ways you will be disappointed by people is very broad. I learn new ways each year. One of the routine ways is when an associate leaves your team or the company. Dozens of Cerner associates I worked with very closely disappointed me by leaving Cerner. Each of them left for a different reason. Each one was a loss for Cerner and impacted me directly.

As a manager, you work with and for people. People will be both rewarding and disappointing. I found a poem attributed to Mother Teresa of Calcutta entitled, *The Final Analysis.* Whether she wrote it or not, I don't know, but I think it captures something of the spirit you need to have when you work with people:

People are often unreasonable, illogical and self-centered;
Forgive them anyway.
If you are kind, people may accuse you of selfish, ulterior motives;
Be kind anyway.
If you are successful, you will win some false friends and some true enemies;
Succeed anyway.
If you are honest and frank, people may cheat you;

Be honest and frank anyway.
What you spend years building, someone may destroy overnight;
Build it anyway.
If you find serenity and happiness, they may be jealous;
Be happy anyway.
The good you do today, people will often forget tomorrow;
Do good anyway.
Give the world the best you have, and it may never be enough;
Give to the world anyway.
You see, in the final analysis, it is all between you and God;
 It was never between you and them anyway.

My habit is that I try to view anomalous behavior separately from the person. Most people are honest, hardworking, and want to succeed in their endeavors. Ultimately we all make mistakes. I know I do. Mistakes are actually healthy in moderation, because they are our greatest source of learning. They don't call it "trial and error" for nothing.

What Associates Want

We have an advantage in defining what the associates on our teams want in life—just answer the question for yourself, and then treat your associates accordingly. The basic question of what people want has been addressed by many. From the Bible to Freud, Skinner, and Maslow, there have been ongoing attempts to describe our wants and needs as they relate to our behavior. While this is somewhat esoteric, I believe it creates a foundation on which to develop a management style. Those of us who took Psychology 101 studied Maslow's hierarchy of needs. His theory was that as our basic needs for food, shelter, and security were met, we ascended to higher needs for self-worth and self-esteem.

During the late 1980s and early 1990s, I read several of Stephen Covey's books in which he expanded Maslow's model somewhat. The book that I believe gives you most of his concepts is *The 7 Habits of Highly Effective People*. I have used several elements of Covey's model in forming my core personal habits, as well as for shaping my view of what I believe others want and expect from me as a manager.

What Associates Want, as a Person and as an Associate

To Live

You can assume that most associates are here to earn a living. Their compensation is the major source that provides food, shelter, clothing, transportation, and long-term security for their families. All of this is extremely important.

As a manager, their careers are in your hands. Be responsible. Be fair. It is very important.

To Love

People want and need to be social, to be appreciated and appreciate others. I always enjoyed seeing the interaction between Cerner associates (and their families) at picnics, volunteer functions, sporting events, and parties. Volunteering for First Hand, getting the kids together for Trunk-or-Treat, competing in Corporate Challenge, or reaching out to others through the "Heart of Cerner" are all ways of letting people be people and serve other needs at the same time. Activities like these build the enriching relationships that make Cerner a fun and caring place. As a manager, you should make sure that your new team members are aware of these and other non-essential but meaningful activities.

It has always spoken volumes to me that, across Cerner, you meet associates who esteem Cerner enough to want their spouses, friends, brothers, sisters, and even children to come to work for Cerner. I don't know what our ratio of "two-Cerner households" is, but I suspect it is high. Of course, some associates have even met their spouses at Cerner.

That leaves room for another, more delicate topic. When the desire "to love" is equated to romantic relationships, you as a manager must be extremely conscientious about maintaining a professional environment for all associates on your team. The workplace is an environment where consensual relationships, both appropriate and inappropriate, will form. One way workplace relationships become inappropriate is when they affect the quality of decisions being made. As a manager, you need to work with your Human Resources Partner to manage the situation and transfer one of the involved associates to another part of Cerner whenever this occurs, and it will occur! Do not procrastinate.

To Learn

My beautiful mother took a computer course not that many years ago. As long as we have our mental health, we will pursue knowledge. Our job is one of the major parts of our lives where we should be and want to be constantly learning. As a manager, recognize this, and challenge your teams to grow their knowledge and skills. Challenge them to be broad, not just deep; that is, if you are managing a technical team, make sure that they are learning about how healthcare works.

To Be Led

Look at the way we elect our government leaders. It is quite an unpleasant and divisive process. After the election, however, no matter whether our guy or gal won or lost, we go back to our lives.

This is because we know that someone must be in charge. I went through years of denial and reflection on this subject. With only a few exceptions, people *want* someone to be in charge. It just so happens that we also have extraordinary expectations of anyone who is leading us.

As the manager, you are in charge. Live up to the expectations of your associates. Expectations will be high.

To Belong

At the neighborhood party, you meet the new neighbor, and within the first ten minutes, the neighbor asks, "What do you do?" Everyone in the room wants to be able to answer that question proudly.

To Be a Winner

Everybody wants to win. Just look at the universally fanatical behavior toward sports, no matter whether it's on the professional, college, high school, or Little League level. If your kid is on the team, you feel better if the team wins. Admit it. Business competition is fierce. We want to win every battle and destroy our competitors. Our victories are very important. Stop and celebrate the major ones. Throw the party. Give the speech. You are the coach.

Personal victories are important, too. When an associate does something outstanding, acknowledge it. I am very disturbed by Cerner managers who cannot seem to place this task very high on their priority list. So much of what we do to retain associates is expensive. Recognition is free, and is much more powerful. A word of praise can do wonders. Jack Welch, former CEO of GE, was known for handwritten notes. Write one and send it to the associate's home. His or her entire family will no doubt read it and be proud. If the deserving associate doesn't work for your team, take the time to write a brief note to the associate's manager. Your words may not be perfect. They don't have to be. I guarantee they will be remembered.

Make sure that you praise the high-performing associates on your team to your own managers, too. Whether out of insecurity or personal ambition, some managers are tempted to steal recognition from their associates. Rather than passing along praise, they take personal credit for the achievements of the high-performing associates on their teams. This unethical behavior damages the trust of associates. Remember that you are the little "*i*" in *i*T. Your team members are the big "T." You are responsible for your team members, developing their skills, growing their careers, and helping them realize their personal goals and objectives.

To Leave a Legacy

Finally, most all of us are motivated to do good and leave the world a better place. One of the things that I liked the best on the farm was being able to see the results of my labor at the end of the day or season. Plowing from sunrise to sunset, smelling the freshly turned earth, and finishing a field were all very satisfying. The seasons drove the activity: plant in the fall, harvest in the early summer, and prepare the fields for next year's crops during the summer. In farming, nature's seasons created a repetitive cycle to our work.

At Cerner, our work and efforts are cumulative. Our success makes us stronger and closer to realizing our vision. Our work affects the quality of healthcare for millions of people around the world. I truly believe that at Cerner, we are leaving this world a better place through our work. As a manager, you must be able to communicate this fact and instill the sense of satisfaction that it creates in your associates.

——————————— **CHAPTER FIVE** ———————————

What Associates Want, as a Team Member

The team wants to know what is necessary to win. They want a plan that coordinates all of the team members and clearly identifies what it means to cross the finish line together. They want to be around other talented, motivated associates working toward the same purpose.

In addition, the team wants decisions to be made quickly and correctly. In other words, they want you to be a great manager.

What Associates *Do Not* Want

Each person on your team is unique, with a personal set of aspirations and ambitions, but also a personal set of dislikes. In my experience there are a few management styles or situations that will be universally resisted by smart, ambitious associates.

Micromanagement

One afternoon in the late 1980s, it struck me that Dr. W. Edwards Deming was still speaking publicly, and that at some point, he would have to get off the road. At that time, he was well into his nineties. I was at his next public lecture. He was clearly a legend and an icon for quality, and I was pumped about the opportunity. I was not disappointed. This man had some extremely strong opinions on a number of subjects. One lesson that he taught was how many managers fundamentally make the mistake of micromanagement.

To illustrate, he used the scenario of giving someone directions for how to go to the airport: I can either give them a map with their current location and the location of airport, and let them use their experience and intelligence to get to the airport, or I can try to give them detailed instructions to go 120 yards, turn right, stay on the highway for 20.3 miles, turn left, and so on. His point was that if you leave out any detail, such as stop at the traffic light if it is red, the "micro" instructions become a disaster.

Give people your expectations and let them surprise you. They will enjoy it much more, and you will have more time to do other things.

Abuse

Some managers attack the person instead of the behavior. Associates will sometimes deliver results for an abusive manager, but only for a time. When they get the chance, they will vote with their feet. Bottom line, treat others as you wish to be treated.

I have a very direct management style. I attack issues, problems, and behaviors—often in a public way. I ask difficult questions of people who are accountable for given areas. When I do so, I am in pursuit of the facts and solutions. These inquiries can create discomfort, tension, conflict, and even confrontation. They can also reveal solutions.

I believe there is a very clear distinction between being aggressive or direct and being abusive. The abusive manager attacks and berates the person, not the behavior. The abusive manager's standard operating mode is one of dissecting and demeaning people rather than solving problems.

I once held onto a highly talented, top-level manager who was abusive to associates. I have since apologized in public on a number of occasions. It was not hard to see the problem, but the executive's skill matched an extraordinary challenge we faced. I received a wake-up call when I found out that his behavior had inspired a saying among associates: "Abuse, Abuse,

Truce, Produce." No matter how much I worked with the executive, his behavior, under stress, became intolerable to his team and others around him.

If you are an executive, it is important to watch for signs that abuse is occurring. Usually you will be the last to know. If you are hearing rumors, become a detective and get the evidence. Once you know the facts, counsel the offender about their behavior, and lay out the "no tolerance" expectation for change. If that doesn't work, fire them or relieve them of having responsibility for people. Above all, make sure the offender is not you.

Change

I mentioned earlier the plaque a physician sent me in the early eighties that reads, *People Fear Change More Than They Do Disaster*. This is true for our associates as well as our clients. Interestingly, our basic business is to purvey change. You will find "managing change" to be one of your great challenges.

How To Build a High-Performance Team

The key to high-performance teams is great leadership and a great team. As a manager, you are responsible for both. Get it right.

The First Step: Hire Right

Hire intelligence and great attitudes—these attributes cannot be changed. There is too much hard work to do for us to hire associates who are not bright enough to do it. Life is too short to work around people with poor attitudes. Beware the candidate with a long resume, who is constantly changing jobs—and notice how frequently he or she claims to be the victim of someone else's mistakes.

Promote the Rising Stars

Here I comment on a tendency I have been noticing in recent years at Cerner. As we mature as a company, it seems that we are less willing to take the risk on emerging talent. When selecting associates to fill new business opportunities, I increasingly hear, "It's too early," "They're too inexperienced," or "That person isn't ready for that level of responsibility." That is nonsense. As a matter of fact, Paul, Cliff, and I were too inexperienced when we started Cerner. In a bigger company, we wouldn't have been considered for the jobs we had just created for ourselves. We took a chance, we worked hard, and Cerner grew. Looking to the next 25 years, we have tremendous opportunities for growth, but it will require taking some chances on talent and potential. If you keep stars from rising, then you are a poor manager who is hurting Cerner. Take a risk. Promote early. You can tell the stars. They will make some mistakes, but you will be in awe of what they *can* do.

In a related concept, groom high-potential associates on your team to fill roles currently occupied by top performers. Encourage meaningful knowledge transfer and mentoring between top talent and the associates who are likely to take their places. That way, you will be better prepared to promote top performers into other roles when their time comes.

Be Clear About the Requirements for a Promotion

The other thing that you must do is be candid with your associates about what they must do to be promoted. Cover this explicitly in your annual interview, write it down, create a personalized plan for your associate. Be honest with them if they are not going to advance to the next level. If they have achieved it, uphold your end of the deal and promote them, even if that means they have to leave your team.

CHAPTER FIVE

Promote From Within

Hiring from the outside, versus promoting within, increases the odds of having incompetent managers in our organization due to lack of alignment with our vision. Paradoxically, promoting rising stars from within can *also* result in having managers who are incompetent—usually due to inexperience. So which is right? Outsiders can bring a fresh new perspective to accomplishing our mission, but I have come to believe that promoting rising stars early is a good thing and is generally worth the risk. As a growing company, we have hired and will hire a great number of people with prior experience. Every time we do so, however, we must first exhaust the internal candidates.

Prune the Tree

The law of large numbers will ultimately make Cerner average unless we have the discipline to remove the poorest performers from our organization. We want an organization that consistently produces future leaders. At Cerner, we have determined that the natural path of a Cerner associate should be to move *UP* into a management role, to move *ACROSS* to bring knowledge to another part of Cerner, to *PRODUCE* consistent and high-quality results in a static role, or to become an *EXPERT* in a given area. *All promotions should be based on merit, not on length of service.* Associates who do not follow the *UP*, *ACROSS*, *PRODUCE*, or *EXPERT* paths should follow a fifth path: *OUT* the door. This may sound blunt, but we would prefer to invest the same time and expense into a future producer, leader, or expert who will bring a higher degree of value to clients, associates, and shareholders.

As I first mentioned in the section on "Edge" in Chapter 1, never transfer the associate who is not performing well in his or her current role. Instead, remove the associate from Cerner. I consider it to be the mark of an extremely poor manager to transfer out a poor performing associate. *Note of exception: In rare cases, I believe in "re-potting" the quality individual who seems to have much to offer the company but is obviously in the wrong role. In these cases, you must have a very honest discussion of the associate's strengths and weaknesses with the hiring manager, so that together you can decide whether the associate will thrive in the new "pot." My rule of thumb is to re-pot twice within Cerner but not a third time—if after two attempts the associate still isn't working out, it's time to let your competitor hire them.*

On an ongoing basis, rank your associates according to performance and potential. This can be difficult, because we relate to the associates on our teams as people, not numbers. This necessary evaluation should be based on both current performance and estimated future capabilities. When formal evaluation time comes, heavily reward the top performers, and promote them quickly. The performance-weighted rewards system helps ensure that the best performers stay at Cerner, and it incents others to raise the bar on their own performance. At the opposite end of the spectrum, notify associates who are struggling to pull their weight that their professional futures are in jeopardy if they keep on their current path. Be specific; clearly describe what is necessary to improve and reach the level of performance expected. Once you have given fair opportunity for improvement, release marginal or low performers from Cerner. It is unfair to ask other members of your team to work with associates who create issues because of their performance. Pruning is necessary to protect a healthy working environment.

Lead by Example

When you manage a team, you are always on stage. Your actions are more important than your words. Outperform everyone on your team. You are setting the standard.

CHAPTER FIVE

Measure *i*T

Associates want to know the measurements so they can understand and attain success. What good is a football game with no score? One of our objectives is to hire high-potential, ambitious associates. These types of associates want to attain and exceed the score. Measurements will drive the activities and culture of an organization. An organization measuring quantity of output may get significantly different activities than one measuring quality of output. The art is to strike the proper balance in the measurements (a balanced scorecard). Either way you cannot manage what you do not measure, and your associates want to understand how they will be measured and how they are doing against these measures.

****

How you take care of the associates on your team will shape Cerner's future. You will find that managing people will be the largest paradox of your career—the source of your greatest joys...and your deepest disappointments.

It is *i*T.

Chapter Six

Managing the Other Ps: Projects, Processes, & Property

The shortest distance between two points is under construction.
– Noelie Alito

The ultimate inspiration is the deadline.
– Nolan Bushnell

While managing people is at the nexus of management, there are a number of other possible management responsibilities and concepts. At the top of the list of others are projects, processes, and property.

Managing Projects

For those busy project managers who have skipped straight to this section of the book, I will repeat what I have already stated: *The art of project management is in starting and…finishing.* A huge mistake I see managers make is not getting the project organized and started quickly. It is as if everyone thinks that there is plenty of time at the end of the project. Wrong. Time is linear. There is just as much time at the beginning. Finishing is very difficult and messy, because there is always an awkward period at the end of the project when it is difficult to determine whether to quit or keep working.

The science of project management is the planning, execution, and control of the project, that is to say, the project work plans, schedules, critical path analyses, and status reports. *Project managers, forget my "do not micromanage" rule.* The key to successful project management is to make sure every project member knows each day what they must do before they go home. And they do it. This is not the same as telling everyone the final date by which major milestones of the project must be completed. If you are assigning a member of your team more than one week of work at a time, then you are not doing your job as a manager. As a project manager, you must make sure team members know all of the tasks they must complete that week, and you must set the expectation that team members will work extra hours and the weekend, if necessary, to achieve the immediate goals.

Here are the four biggest enemies to a successful project:

1. *Not controlling project scope. If scope is constantly changing or never defined, then there is no real plan, and there is no hope of delivering a project on time and on budget. This is one of the only ways I use the word* budget. **The art of controlling project scope is saying NO!** *Everyone wants to please the client. However, a project that is late and over budget will definitely not please the client. The client will not remember that they changed the scope; all they will remember is that we are late and over budget.*

2. *Not having an effective framework for getting accurate, timely decisions made. The lack of effective and timely decision-making kills the productivity of the entire project and results in significant rework and huge losses of productivity.*

3. *Not having adequate, committed, competent, full-time resources. Any good project manager knows that he or she wants full control over all key resources. Without it, your critical project resources will be working on other, unknown priorities.*

4.*Poor project management skills. As a manager, this is your area. I do not want to be repetitive: Project management is having a good plan, writing it down, communicating the plan to all parties, executing well, having a control system, and publishing its status frequently. The plan must be specific for each project member, and no task assigned to an individual should ever be more than one week of work. More than one week, and you will not be able to determine the progress of the project member. As a project manager, you must know what everyone is working on and their status. At the end of each week, every project member must provide an "estimate to complete" (hours remaining) for all open tasks. The project plan should be updated with the new estimates each week. If your deadline is in jeopardy, take action quickly.*

Managing Processes

Processes are the glue that connects the parts of an organization, synchronizing associates, teams, and organizational units. Externally, processes are the reliable connections between the enterprise and its clients and business partners. The goal of business process development is to be able to efficiently create a predefined set of tasks that produce a highly repeatable set of results. At the beginning of my career, the term was procedure, not process. I actually prefer to use the term *system*, because it is more of a top-down, comprehensive view of how the various parts of an organization connect and interact. I grew up managing projects; most of them were to build systems for clients. Probably the biggest difference between projects and processes is that projects have start and stop dates, while business processes are continuous. When managing a project, you develop a specific project plan for a project team. It is all very tangible, with a finish line. I have always felt that it is easier to motivate a team toward a specific date and set of objectives.

Growth obsoletes business processes. My rule of thumb is that 50 percent growth of an organization will usually obsolete current-state processes. *Note: Cerner has doubled in size every two to three years for most of its first 25 years. Apply the rule of thumb, and you will see how challenged we have been to keep our business processes operating well.*

The new volume clogs current-state processes that used to work under less stress, exposing their inefficiencies and lack of scalability. A smaller organization lives off of tacit (undocumented) knowledge to keep things going. The larger an organization becomes, the greater the need to have formal processes defined. With rapid growth comes a strong sense that there is no available time to think about processes or make changes because everyone is really busy, which is the opposite of how the effective manager should think. It is the growth that makes it imperative that you expect to have to redesign how the work is done. One result of failing to rethink processes is that you start to lose very good associates because of increasing stress and chaos inside your organization.

I discovered early in my Cerner experience that very good project managers are many times not good managers of process. I was perplexed with this because most of the projects we do are to build and implement systems in business and clinical process environments. To be good at that, you must be competent to understand organizational processes. That is the essence of our work. For years, our mission statement was *To Automate the Process of Managing Healthcare*. I have never developed a theory about why there is such a big difference between project managers and process managers, but rather have concluded that some people enjoy designing or building a machine, and others enjoy operating or maintaining the machine. I became sensitive to this difference as Cerner grew and we were building the management team. The fact is, we need both types of managers. Interestingly, some managers are excellent at both. Much of our front-line, client-facing activity is project work. Software engineering is really a hybrid, combining both project and process. Clearly, the internal operations of Cerner depend greatly on effective business processes.

The keys to good organizational process, whether internal or in a client environment, are as follows:

- Start with the client's objective. The most common mistake I see is for organizations to design process around getting the team's or unit's work done efficiently and without error. This is not our mission. We are here to deliver value to our clients. Everything we do must relate back to them.

- Handoffs kill. The pass-off of work between teams or other business units will be the weakest link in any process. This is where things fall through the cracks, priorities are altered, and errors of all kind occur.

- Automate processes wherever possible. Machines do the same thing every time — humans do not, resulting in variance. Humans have judgment, machines do not. Automate processes for things machines are good at, and keep a human involved for the parts that require judgment. A prerequisite to automation is understanding the processes. I often see people attempting to automate processes before they understand the processes, which is a recipe for failure.

- Measure, measure, measure. For every key process, you must measure the error rates, the efficiency (inputs versus outputs), the profitability (where applicable), and the satisfaction of the major stakeholders (typically associates and clients, both internal and external).

- Continuously improve. Deming was right. The key to quality is continuously improving core processes. Take action to improve the error rates, efficiency, profitability, and satisfaction. The data (measurements) will be your light. Your team will be the source of your ideas. You are the manager: improve *i*T.

Managing Quality

As a manager, process is your lever to produce quality in your organization. The concept of quality can be very vague, however, and initially does not present itself in your windshield of things requiring your immediate attention. The impact of poor quality does present itself, dramatically and repeatedly. How should a manager specifically approach quality? Because quality and process are so closely related, there should be a good deal of overlap between your approach to managing the two things. I believe there are five very specific *it*s to managing quality:

Embed It

Nothing starts with quality. Instead, it starts with an idea, motion, confusion, and chaos. Quality is pride at the beginning. Deming agreed by saying that quality is "pride in workmanship." Make quality part of your team's culture. It is a function of the skills and personal attributes of our associates, managers, and leaders. At the end, it is all only about quality.

Define It

As a manager, you have the brunt of the responsibility here. A number of years ago, I defined the "Abilities" for Intellectual Property (IP) and Intellectual Capital (IC), the two core areas creating Cerner's value. Please note that you define quality starting from the clients' eyes. Never define quality based on internal criteria.

The IP Abilities

Marketable	Usable	Reliable	Manageable
Affordable	Performable	Securable	Serviceable
Scaleable	Flexible	Predictable	Maintainable
Measureable	Available	Accessible	Upgradeable
Transformable	Installable	Auditable	Adaptable
	Interface-able		

Figure 6.1 – The IP Abilities

Assign It

I then assigned responsibility for each of the Abilities. There must be clarity before there is responsibility. Likewise, there must be responsibility before there can be accountability.

Cerner Abilities

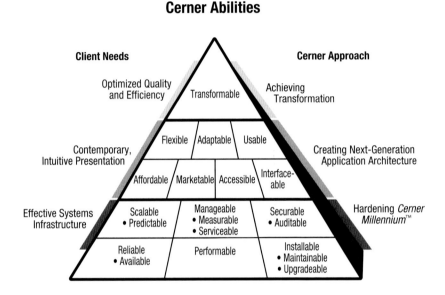

Figure 6.2 – Technical Architecture's Abilities Slide

The Technical Architecture organization converted their assigned Abilities into the pyramid pictured above in Figure 6.2, and used it to drive a great deal of work on hardening the architecture of *Cerner Millennium*.

Measure It

Only after you define it should you invest in measuring it. As I noted in Chapter 3, "Plan, Execute, & Control", be careful in choosing your metrics. It is tempting to choose metrics that are easy to achieve and that make your team look good on a graph, but in the end, will those metrics really correspond to success in your plan? Again, the value of results to the clients must be inherent in the measurement. We are now guaranteeing 99.9 percent system *availability* (one of the Abilities), subject to conditions, to our clients, changing the competitive landscape in our industry.

System Availability

System Availability [%]	99%	99.9%	99.99%	99.999%
Hours System Unavailable	87.6	8.8	0.9	Rounds to Zero

Figure 6.3 – Improving Availability

Improve It

Continually pursue how to improve the current state. When I talk with clients about our unprecedented 99.9 percent system availability guarantee, I indicate that that is not good enough and clearly state that our goal is 99.999 percent availability. Do the math; there are 8,760 (365x24) hours in one year.

What availability does healthcare deserve? If your child's life is at stake, which column do you want to achieve? We must improve.

You have highly talented members on your team. Create a culture of quality, embed it, define it, assign it, measure it, and improve it. You will be impressed with your team's creativity.

Managing Property

If you own a rock, it needs managing. If it has value, you need to make sure it is secure, probably insure it. When the local government learns of its value, you will pay property taxes on it. If it is part of a collection, you will want to display it. If it is on your balance sheet, the auditors will want to inventory it. Now in the era of the Sarbanes-Oxley Act, the auditors will want you to hire consultants to review the controls around the inventory procedures and probably want to conduct the inventory annually.

Cerner divides property into two categories, intellectual and physical. The management of intellectual property (IP)—architecture, software, knowledge content, patents, trademarks, and copyrights—is a great topic, an important one that is unfortunately outside the scope of this book. Maybe I will write a book called *Manage IP*. I bet you can't wait.

That leaves physical property. Every organization has a physical side: the offices, the furniture, and in some cases the fleets. The physical side of our organization is extremely important, both externally to clients and internally to associates. It is often the first impression clients and others have of us, and it is a significant part of their view of Cerner. Internally, the physical side of our organization also has a direct effect on the productivity of the majority of our associates.

At Cerner, we have always had two distinct environments: *on stage* and *backstage*. Each of these environments has its own importance.

On Stage

We believe that clients' perceptions of our organization are strongly influenced by our physical appearance, both human and property. As a result, we design and manage the visible portion of Cerner knowing that it is always on stage and part of the show. This takes a commitment of valuable resources and impacts our bottom line. But the expenditure produces a positive return for our shareholders and allows us to invest more in the research and development of solutions that advance our role and mission in healthcare.

Here are a couple of quick stories about these *on stage* commitments.

Our Front Door

The six original buildings in the North Kansas City, Missouri, Rockcreek campus were built as "spec" buildings to rent in small spaces to individual tenants such as Cerner. Our presence on campus evolved as we went from renting only 5,000 square feet in the southeast corner of the 6th floor of the 2800 building in 1981 to purchasing the entire campus in 1994.

It was over the Christmas holiday in 1999 that I first focused on not having a front door or a sign on our property that identified it as the Cerner campus. It took me a full 20 years after founding Cerner to notice—obviously physical presence was not a high priority for a startup company. This realization occurred as I pondered the future competition that would come from large, multinational companies with household brand names that were recognizable by any client's board of directors. It seemed intuitive to remedy this situation. In doing so, we created a unique Cerner front door with a 188-foot abstract representation of nature's double helix, which makes up the human genome and programs all living things with the sequence of four chemicals: adenine, cytosine, guanine, and thymine. Surrounding the double helix of the Cerner Spire is a representation of the digital code that we use to make machines smart. This binary code is represented by 1s and 0s. What a door to our stage! What a message to our future clients.

The Vision Center

We have long recognized that one of our largest marketing challenges is that the core value we offer to clients, our software, is invisible. It was imperative that we represent to our client *what* our software did in their environments and how it creates value to their organizations.

To do so, we needed to create a facsimile of our clients' environments. The Cerner Vision Center opened in April of 1992. It has been a great investment.

Since its inception, the Vision Center is highly recognized in our industry; nearly all of our competitors have tried to replicate it. They are fearful when a prospective client comes to the Vision Center, knowing that Cerner's chances for success have just increased; consequently, they try to disparage it, a sure sign of its effectiveness. One competitor calls their imitation the "Reality Center." The Vision Center is a great example of how physical property can reveal the value of intellectual property.

The Associate Center

Our future is totally dependent on the quality of our associates. After seeing the success of the Vision Center, we decide to build our second center, the Associate Center. At a companywide Town Hall in 1992, I announced our intent to build a center for our associates that included major recreational and child care facilities. I confessed that there were some details that would have to be worked out, including the fact that we did not own the land where we wanted to put the building. It was this announcement that emphasized our need to negotiate the purchase of our 88-acre property in North Kansas City. The Associate Center is a great example of how physical property can support the health of our Intellectual Capital, the part of Cerner that goes home each day in the minds of our associates.

Backstage

The *backstage* areas of Cerner are different, but they are no less important. The physical environments must support the productivity of our associates and facilitate collaborative behavior. Each is an area where the triangle of conflict between shareholders, associates, and clients is clearly seen. Each Cerner associate would like to have a personal office and assistant. Our clients would like to see all of our investment go into capabilities that support their today problems and needs. Our shareholders would like to see our investments go into growing the top line and margins *today*.

At Cerner, our biggest investment in productivity and teamwork is to wire Cerner to achieve connectivity and coordination. We have had a ratio of more than one interactive computing device per associate since the mid-1990s. Our core universal business applications are e-mail and enterprisewide scheduling. Before Outlook and Meeting Place, we had our own internally developed applications (MOV for messaging and CTM for scheduling). First the local networks, then the Internet, broadband, and now the wireless networks have added new, exciting dimensions to our connectivity, communication, and coordination, changing the fundamental productivity of any organization.

The workspace is a very important variable that directly impacts productivity, communication, and connectivity within our organization. Cerner managers must carefully consider its impact, which I actually believe is more significant than any org chart. The individual's workspace directly impacts productivity and that of the collective team. The reason I am not a big fan of the home as the primary work site is because that environment isolates the individual from the rest of the organization and has all of the interruptions of daily living—dogs to be fed, kids needing attention, workers wanting to fix the dishwasher. The second major consideration is the *coffee pot effect*. A great deal of important ad hoc communication happens informally as associates bump into one another while away from their desks. Many business problems are solved in the informal, chance meetings of the right two or three associates. Although we are constantly experimenting with alternatives, most designs of our physical work environments have been based on the team.

A manager must think about the best use of physical assets. Keep a clear idea of what you are trying to accomplish. Beware of making decisions based on how you did things in the past. Make sure you are thinking beyond the present.

A Bonus: Managing Your "Boss" and Your Career

Managers of people, projects, property, and processes: I am including this bonus section on managing your boss and your career for everybody. I considered placing this with the chapter on managing people, but I decided it would get better attention on its own.

Managing Your Boss

All of us do not manage people, but all of us have bosses. (I send my self-appraisal to Cerner's Board of Directors each year.) By adding this as a separate section, I am not trying to imply that bosses are not people. *Note: Boss isn't my favorite word in many contexts, but I am going to use it here because it's the word we all tend to use when informally talking about our own managers.*

The idea of managing your boss may seem odd, but I believe your career will be better if you figure out this skill. My basic assumption is that you are highly motivated, intelligent, and excellent in your role, and one day you will be the CEO of Cerner. To speed your progress, then, I want to share several things I learned from my experiences on both sides of the associate/boss equation. Because your boss will be a manager of managers, they will have to make important choices about where to focus their time and attention. Below are some thoughts that will make you a hero.

Consistently Deliver the Results— Make Your Boss a Hero

You will be loved if you consistently deliver great results. Early in my career, my projects were delivered on time and without write-offs. Guess what? I was never unassigned. The partners fought for me to be on their projects because I made them look good.

Do Your Job AND Your Boss's Job

There is nothing better than to have associates working for you who are always three steps ahead of you. The key to doing this successfully is to change your context. Think about your job—and theirs—from your boss's context. Once you are done with your job, do theirs. You will be amazed how quickly your career moves.

Allow the Boss To Contribute

This was one of the first things I had to learn when working with partners at Arthur Andersen. Sooner of later, the partner will show up at the engagement. They feel a strong need to contribute something of value when they show up. It is basic human nature to contribute. You will be amazed at how relaxed your boss will become once his or her contribution is seen as a good idea AND your project is on schedule and under budget. You may also find their ideas helpful.

Be a "No Problem" Manager

Problems always happen. Just solve them. If you are the naysayer who always predicts gloom and doom, then no one will want to have you as part of a team. There are always plenty of problems, and some of them even warrant briefing your manager. The key, however, is to *present the answer* to the problem at the same time you present the problem. If you present the problem only, then you really are trying to hand it to your boss to solve. I assure you that your career is limited if you have those tendencies.

Likewise, learn to avoid picking up "bonus" problems from the members of the team you manage. William Oncken, Jr., and Donald L. Wass wrote about this concept in a 1974 *Harvard Business Review* article, "Management Time: Who's Got the Monkey?" Later Oncken and Ken Blanchard used the same concept in a book they co-authored in *The One Minute Manager* series. They recommend for you as manager to view the people walking into your office as having monkeys on their backs. In the end, anyone who leaves after describing the problem without the solution has just left that monkey on your back. Soon, you will have an entire office full of monkeys. Offer your support when it is warranted, but know that the *best* support is often encouraging the associates on your team to solve their own problems.

Never Make Your Boss Do Your Job

Without a doubt, the worst thing you can do is to make your boss do your job. While this situation could occur for a number of reasons, the two most common reasons that I have had to do someone else's job have been instances when I have had to make the decision to replace an associate (rather than the person's boss making the decision), and times when I have had to step in to repair an inadequate relationship of sales or consulting leadership with senior client management.

You do not want your boss to decide to replace your team members. This means that you have forced your boss to deal with the consequences of your lack of edge, lack of judgment, or inappropriate loyalty to an individual at the expense of the company. All of these reasons are serious black marks on your management record.

In the second most common scenario, one more applicable to the client side of our company, you do not want to force your boss to tend and mend client relationships that you could have been tending yourself. When the local sales or engagement teams do not develop relationships with the client's executive team, this is a signal to me that there is a lack of maturity, professionalism, or self confidence within the local management team. The most common excuse I hear from our local team is, "But the CIO blocks me from contacting the rest of the management team." Have I given you my thoughts on excuses yet? Suffice it to say that this one doesn't fly. Conversely, nothing impresses me as a boss more than seeing young Cerner associates develop strong relationships with our clients' senior management teams.

Have a Backbone

If there are five of us in a room and we all agree, then four of us are providing no value. Do not be a "yes" person. If you disagree, speak up. Take a chance and make your argument. The best idea is the thing we are after, and that seldom comes from the highest-ranking person in the room. At Cerner, we value ideas, not titles.

When presenting your case, follow the Cerner philosophy of courteous aggressive action. Be respectful, but make your case. Another absolute Cerner rule: *If you oppose, you must propose.* Your style of disagreeing says a lot about you as a person and as a manager. Make sure the message is a good one. We need a culture of open-minded, talented managers and associates who respectfully allow others to speak up.

Managing Your Career

In the same way that all of us have bosses, we also all have careers. Cerner's vision continues to create high-quality, organic growth, one in which management opportunities will abound. As a company, we need careers that have steep vectors. To be promoted, be a star who consistently delivers results, and you will make the short list when we are looking for the management team that will create the next version of Cerner. If you want to advance quickly, here is my advice to you.

Create Your Replacement

The number one reasons high-performing associates are not promoted is that there is no replacement for them on their team. *You are responsible for growing your replacement.* Do *i*T.

You Manage It

Do not expect anyone else to manage your career. It is yours. Managers manage, so manage your career. Create your plan, and update it at least annually.

Manage Your Network

From day one, you will be building a network of contacts inside Cerner. Make it part of your professional annual plan to continue to refresh and grow your network in a 360-degree fashion. Your network must reach to *all* parts of the company, not just your organization. It also will extend and needs to extend into our client organizations and industry.

Cerner makes a huge investment in trying to start all careers in the United States at our World Headquarters, even when the role is a virtual one. College and early career recruits must spend at least two years developing in Kansas City in close contact with other associates. We want all Cerner associates to have a peer group that crosses all parts of the company. There is a huge difference in the way an engineer responds to a consultant's question, based on whether he or she has a personal relationship with the associate. The best way to create a strong network is for you to be the resource to others. Then, when you are the one needing help, it comes quickly and willingly.

****

I must stop this chapter here. Not because I have reached any limits of either the breadth or depth of defining your possible responsibilities as a manager, but for practicality's sake. I have an impulse to try to communicate my understanding and beliefs on many other management topics that are relevant to Cerner, such as the economics of software, the mechanics of our business model; managing large-scale architectures; managing innovation; managing culture; managing software developers; managing core business functions such as human resources, finance, marketing and business systems; and my favorite topics of leadership and entrepreneurship. To write about these worthy concepts *now* would unnecessarily delay our companywide discussion of what it means to be a good manager.

To me, business is fun. It is constantly changing, it challenges your intelligence, it is highly competitive, it rewards the winners and punishes the losers, and most importantly, it is the foundation of our way of life and is the source of the innovation and advances that improve the quality of our lives. You will never master your management role. Join me in a lifelong pursuit of the subject.

Chapter Seven

From Sand to Gems: Management Pearls

He was a bold man that first eat an oyster.
– Jonathan Swift

I sometimes relate to an oyster. Not a very glamorous comparison, I know, but this seldom-seen invertebrate has two properties I admire and want to emulate. First, an oyster has a hard shell that shields it from its environment and predators. Second, inside the protection of its shell, the oyster can take a miniscule grain of sand and turn it into a pearl.

In my journey, I have accumulated a string of pearls—maxims and insights that I use almost daily in viewing my responsibilities as a manager. I have collected these in a variety of ways: reflecting on my own experience, reading the written thoughts of others, listening to others, and using my powers of observation. I offer my string of pearls to you, knowing very well that what I consider to be jewels may to you be glass beads.

The topics in this chapter represent somewhat complex thoughts. Whereas most of this book is very simple and straightforward, to get the full benefit of this chapter, you may have to think a little.

Think Top-Down, Bottom-Up

Somewhere along the line, I adopted a particular way of looking at opportunities, challenges, issues, and problems. I call it "top-down, bottom-up." If you are trying to fix something that is broken, you need to first identify where to focus your efforts. The application of this principle is not limited to diagnosing business problems within your organization, however. It also applies to creative disciplines such as designing a new software solution for a market. When you think about it, every opportunity is the result of a problem.

As you can tell by now, I am big on developing strong habits around knowing where to start. In Chapter 4, "From Vision to Value," I explained the importance of properly sequencing the Vision-to-Value (V^2) algorithm, Vision + Mission + Strategy + Structure + Process + Tools = Results (Attainment, Trend, Variance). In that chapter, I focused on detecting problems by measuring the results. Results trip the alarm. Once the alarm goes off, I have learned to start at the top, not the bottom or middle.

When you are the leader, you are setting direction and priorities for others; it is imperative that you have a complete view of the field in front of you. Always start at the top. You need the biggest picture possible of the issues and opportunities facing your organization. You want to know how your organization's mission fits into the rest of the model. *Never* assume that you understand. This is a source of management mistakes at all levels of management. Things change. At Cerner, the only constant is change.

I have a compelling need to understand the whole model. That is why during most of Cerner's 25-year history, we have had a single picture or graphic model of our vision. Looking at issues and opportunities from the top will create the "flash bulb" revelation of new directions that you want your organization to take. Looking top-down reveals new relationships that you simply cannot find when you are working in the details. I am sure that this is the meaning behind the old expression, "...can't see the forest for the trees." Initially, I am uninterested in the details, because I know that the details will consume all of my oxygen once I start to work on them.

Once I have the big picture clearly in mind and can communicate it, however, I convert and work the issue from the bottom. The bottom is dominated by CCC: chaos, confusion, and complexity. If you are investigating an issue of any scale, there might be many person-years of effort at the bottom. At Cerner, the bottom requires specific knowledge of an extreme range of possible topics—the depths of information technology, Cerner architecture, the science of clinical medicine, the subtleties of healthcare delivery organizations—all in the context of how Cerner's organization currently operates. The front-line manager has been immunized from the CCC long ago and in many cases believes that he or she has complete mastery of the bottom. Most managers in the line of command above the bottom have a subliminal awareness of CCC and have learned to avoid touching the bottom.

If your intent is to solve a problem or create something new of value in your clients' universe, however, you *must* touch the bottom, regardless of whether you are the CEO or the front-line manager. Even though that is where CCC lives, you will increase your knowledge and judgment geometrically by touching the bottom. The bottom is where you gain an understanding of the depth and complexity of the issues you are facing and gauge how much effort it will take to implement changes or new directions for your organization. The more you are willing and able to understand the detail, the more success you will find. In making the deep dive, you will also gain your team's confidence and respect.

A common mistake I see inexperienced managers make is that of looking at a problem from a single perspective. They look at things neither from the top nor the bottom, but simply from their customary standpoint, typically somewhere in the middle. Most problems cannot be solved without changing the view. Another mistake I see some managers make is that, when they *do* change positions, they start at the bottom—right in the middle of CCC. Guess what happens? They become infected with the chaos, confusion, and complexity. Now they become carriers, infecting others. Not exactly what you want from managers in your organization. Many of us grew up from the bottom, and as a result we are not afraid to go back there. The bottom has a gravity to it. It is where you naturally end up when pursuing an issue. But working business problems from that bottom only is always suboptimal and in many cases is a fatal mistake.

When you sense chaos, confusion, and complexity, resist your instinct to go deeper. Learn to back up, back off, and look for the big picture. Remember the sequence: top-down, bottom-up.

At one point in our company's history, following a big growth spell, Cerner had a business problem in being unable to plan the financial performance of our rapidly growing Cerner Consulting organization. The leaders of this group were well aware of the issue, and I was clear that the problem needed to be fixed. It was an extremely talented group of managers and executives who, in a prior era, had converted Cerner Consulting from a financial drain to a profitable part of Cerner. I wanted these leaders to diagnose and solve their own problem. These executives also very much wanted to solve this business problem on their own. Their approach was to convene meetings to discuss the issues, study tons of data, and make the list of things they would change. The situation increasingly grew in severity. Quarter after quarter, a pattern emerged. Each quarter, as the variance from "plan" got wider and as the predictability of the results decreased, the meetings would reconvene.

Lists would be generated again, and there would once again be a pronouncement that they had found the problem and that it would start to improve in the next quarter.

The managers' instincts led them to the bottom, where the predictable happened: chaos, confusion, and complexity reigned. Eventually, I decided that I must intervene. They were making one of the most basic management mistakes: There was no real plan. They were confused and thought that they had one. Remember, the basic job of management is to plan, execute, and control. If you don't have a plan, there can be no control; therefore, all you are doing is executing. The "plan" they were working against was actually a prediction. They had built a model in which they predicted revenues based on *how many consultants were on the payroll*. They put in the number of consultants on the payroll multiplied by the expected number of billable hours and realized rates, and the model spit out the expected consulting revenues for the quarter. CCC was having its finest hour at the expense of Cerner shareholders.

Plans must address what actually happens at the execution level (bottom) of the organization. The top-level plan is usually the sum of a series of interlocking plans. What we were missing in this case was the series of plans for *every* client project and plans for *every* associate showing *every* project they would be working on and at what rate.

Building a real plan can be hard. But if you are a manager, it is your responsibility. As CEO, I am the chief manager. In less than one hour, I designed the basic method for building a plan for a consulting organization of more than 1,500 associates. We spent many months ironing out the plan specifics. Once we had a *plan*, the management team and the rest of the organization focused on *execution*. The plan *controls* highlighted where we needed to improve the execution. After the plan's implementation, our consulting organization met or exceeded its plan very consistently. This is the benefit of thinking top-down, bottom-up.

The intent in sharing this story is not to make me sound like a superhero manager, solving something that others had worked on for more than two years in less than one hour. There was nothing complex or heroic about what I did. My point in sharing this is for you to understand, as a manager, that _you_ have the means to tackle enormous problems and be successful. The keys are described in an early passage from this book: "Get calm. Get the big picture. Get organized. Get a plan. Get to work. Quit worrying, and quit thinking someone else is going to tell you how to do this. Just think about it, use your common sense, intelligence, skills, and talents— the strongest potion you will find." This Consulting issue was an important matter for our company. I had been very candid with our Board of Directors about being concerned with this area of our organization for a number of reasons, including the increasing variance it was causing in our corporate plans. I also shared that I knew what to go do if the team didn't learn to solve the problem. In other words I had spent a great deal of time before the one hour...THINKING.

Although I use this story to illustrate the importance of thinking top-down, bottom-up, I also share it to challenge you to think about how you will give and receive input as a manager. All along, I communicated to the top manager, as clearly as I could, my assessment of the problem and the direction I would take in solving it, were I in his position. I cannot tell you why the advice was ignored. It could be the natural instinct of talented people to want to be independent and prove their worth. I assume that part of it was my style. I believe strongly in setting vision, mission, and the direction we are headed. I believe strongly in empowering others to find the path to follow. As I have described to you in this book, I do not like micromanagers, *Command and Control* style, or autocratic forms of management. As a manager, however, you must develop an inner sense of asking: "Right direction or wrong direction?" When the "wrong direction" alarm goes off, you must react and engage. When my own alarm goes off, I have a wide range of responses; most of them are proportionate to the experience level of the managers or teams. In the above case, I was dealing with some of the senior-most managers in the company. Because I had a great deal of confidence in the team and believed Cerner would benefit if they solved this problem, I tried to strike the right balance between hanging back and offering advice.

As a management team, we create a chain of managers managing managers. When you are one of the links in the chain, you need to listen and THINK about what your manager is saying. In many cases, it will be obtuse and not central to your view of the problem. In other cases, it will be contrary to what you believe is the right path to take. There will be a real calculus in how you assimilate the advice. As an intermediate manager, you are not a robot. You *create* and execute the plan for your responsibilities. But you owe your manager a direct response to his or her advice and comments. If you believe your manager is wrong, you must tell him or her so. Make your argument. Most of the time, you will win the argument because you have many more facts. Sometimes you may be surprised to find that there is some real wisdom derived from life experience conveyed in your manager's advice and commentary.

You will find yourself managing others in this type of situation, also. As you get more experience, you will find your "trigger" that causes you to make the tough decision to intervene directly and take over. You are responsible. Managers manage.

Use Principle-Based Values

Along the way, I have found it important to appreciate the differences between principles and values. Principles are defined by natural laws. They cannot be altered. For example, on the farm, you deal with a number of natural laws. You cannot change the weather or the seasons.

Values are defined by individuals, groups, organizations, or as social norms. They are a reflection of what those people esteem. Values can and do change. They change based on the opinions of people. They may be based on true principles, but because they are defined by individuals or organizations, they are not always principle-based.

Principles vs. Values

Principles	Values
■ Natural Law	■ Social Norm
■ Objective	■ Subjective
■ Farm	■ School
■ Leadership	■ Management
■ Factual	■ Emotional

Figure 7.1 – Principles vs. Values

At Cerner, we have for many years listed and explained our *Statement of Values*. The word values is appropriate here, but we have made every attempt to be principle-based in these definitions. An example from this list of values is *Strive and Thrive to Serve Our Clients: Our clients are the stewards of the health of our communities.* Every Cerner manager is to live these values and teach them to every Cerner associate.

Never Forecast With a Ruler

Nothing in nature or business moves in a straight line. Too many times I watch managers forecast the future as though it is merely an extension of the past. In reality, there are always changes in both our internal and external environments that will alter the fundamental slope of the line. The art is to detect the changes in the line's direction. These changes are difficult to detect because, on a month-to-month, quarter-to-quarter, and even year-to-year basis, progress comes in spurts and sputters, creating somewhat of a saw-blade trend line. The art is to anticipate when the slope of the saw shifts and to make adjustments to your plans.

The most painful mistakes in my history at Cerner have been times when I failed to see one of these shifts coming. Although the shifts represent both positive and negative changes in directions, the negative ones are particularly brutal. For instance, your plans typically are to continue to spend at the same rate of change as in the past, which is fine until something happens to affect the top line. By not anticipating the change, all of the variance falls directly to the bottom line, EPS, and cash flow. It is an unpleasant way of learning to forget the ruler when forecasting.

Create Real Value & Good Things Will Happen

The purpose of a business organization is to create value for its clients or customers. The job is far from over with the creation phase, but good things tend to fall into place if you create substantial value for others. To survive, an organization must be able to create something of value at a cost or investment that is, in the long term, less than the payment received back from its clients. That "something" is likely going to be a service, a technology, or a solution. I have long believed that it is important to be able to succinctly articulate your value proposition to your clients.

At Cerner, we propose to eliminate all avoidable medical errors, inappropriate medical variance, unnecessary waste of resources, needless delay of care, and costly administrative friction. This is a huge statement. I think it is the largest value proposition in healthcare. It might be the entrepreneur in me, but I believe that Cerner is on the path to deliver this value to countries, communities, healthcare organizations, and to people in all of the major roles in healthcare. The key stakeholders in a better healthcare system, purchasers (employers and governments) as well as the consumers (us as individuals and families), will also see benefits from this value proposition. If we are successful, good things will happen to Cerner.

"Only the Paranoid Survive"

Andy Grove, longtime chairman and CEO of Intel, is credited with the statement, "Only the paranoid survive." Remember, the previous Intel CEO and founder Gordon Moore is credited with Moore's Law, the observation that semiconductor capacity per dollar cost tends to double in a very short period of time—between one year and 24 months. Moore's Law has accurately predicted the last 40 years of technological development. No wonder Andy was paranoid.

Cerner management must be paranoid. Healthcare is constantly changing, healthcare policy will force major changes in the future, and a growing number of our competitors are highly capitalized and very smart.

With Cerner as the leader in this industry, they are all aiming at the bull's-eye on our back. We will survive in the long term only if we are truly paranoid…because they really are out to get us!

The Art Is in the Timing

The hardest thing about business decisions is knowing when to make one. The bigger the decision, the greater the ambiguity around its timing. I have concluded that *the art of business is in the timing.* If you are too early, you die. If you are too late, you are irrelevant.

In sports, timing is impossible to teach; it must be developed. I believe this is also true in business. Unfortunately, there is precious little I can think to write that can give you any insight on how to make the *right* decision *at the right time.* I can only relate that my biggest decisions (starting Cerner, choosing laboratory as our first major application, moving beyond the lab to create *Health Network Architecture,* pulling the trigger on *HNA Millennium,* and so on) have burnt an impression about the importance of timing into my consciousness. At the time you are making a major decision, the chaos in your environment will accentuate your uncertainty about both the timing and the direction to take. Later, after it is clear that you made the right decision, you will wonder why it took you so long to decide.

It is crucial to be aware of the need for a decision. That is why my weekly plan includes a section called Decide. Once I know a decision is needed, I try to get a clear idea about the triggers that will indicate that it is time to decide. The trigger becomes the alarm that the time is now. The last step is the decision itself. Again, being too early or too late robs much of the value you are trying to create with the decision.

NEAL PATTERSON

With all of that said, do not become gun-shy in making decisions. Usually, it is better to *change* an incorrect prior decision than to miss the right time by *failing* to make a decision. I would rather make 100 major decisions in one year and have to fix 10 of them than to make only 10 perfect decisions.

The Triangle of Conflict

There is an inherent conflict in every decision we make at Cerner. The conflict is between the client, the associate, and the shareholder. To make the case, I will use a theoretical example: Our clients would like to have our IP and services for free. Our associates would like to have their compensation doubled and their hours halved. Our shareholders would like for our clients to pay double and for all of our associates to take a 50 percent pay decrease. While this sounds extreme, it is representative of the constant tension you will face as a manager. As managers, we must simultaneously solve the equation and balance everyone's interests.

The key to successful decision-making is to think of the long-term consequences of decisions, and to remember that if Cerner fails, all three constituents suffer as a result. Clients would have to switch to another solution supplier, enduring significant costs in new licenses, hardware, off-the-shelf components, and project work. All associates would lose their jobs, experiencing, at the very least, a career setback if not worse. Shareholders would lose all of the value of their equity stake in Cerner.

When you think of the long-term consequences, the conflict is easier to reconcile because it *must* be reconciled. Only the short-term issue remains. How, then, do you resolve the conflict in the short term? You don't. It is only with a pattern of decisions focused on the long-term view that you create balance and represent each constituent. For example, the decision to build the Associate Center, made in 1992 and opened in 1994, clearly benefited the Kansas City-based associates, not our clients, shareholders, or even the non-K.C.-based associates. In fact, it clearly added to the corporate overhead. In the short term, the decision caused a little tension. Over a number of years, however, I believe that the Associate Center has contributed to our ability to attract and retain highly talented associates. This in turn has benefited our clients, our shareholders, and the non-KC based Cerner associates. Over time, if you are a good manager, you will create a patchwork of decisions that, in the end, will resemble a quilt. You will make each decision for the short-term benefit of only one of the three constituents, but overall (if done well) there will be a remarkable balance to the pattern.

As managers, our responsibilities also extend beyond the associate, client, and shareholder. First, we must strive to be fair, consistent, and open with our trading partners. Too often, I see managers using fundamentally unfair tactics with our partners, using our size and relative importance to obtain an unjust outcome. This should not be. We also have an implicit responsibility to the countries and communities in which we do business. Finally, because as managers, we have increased knowledge and decision-making power, we have an equally increased responsibility to those with less knowledge and power.

Unfortunately, recent highly publicized corporate failures (Enron, Tyco, WorldCom/MCI, and in our own industry, McKesson/HBOC) have highlighted the emergence of a clear pattern in which management starts managing to benefit management over all others. Individual managers and, more disturbingly, management groups succumb to the temptation to optimize their own personal interests over all other stakeholders. This is a bad situation, usually indicating a decaying company ready for a big fall. Companies die from the top down.

Plant a Tree Today

When is the best time to plant a tree? Answer: Twenty-five years ago. When is the next best time to plant a tree? Answer: Today.

I wake up each morning with the attitude that, as a manager, "I manage from this point forward." I cannot change the past. Yes, I know that's profound.

Every tree I plant today and tomorrow can significantly enhance our future two, five, ten, and twenty years from now. Twenty-five years ago, Cliff, Paul, and I planted a little tree, and we have since planted many trees at Cerner. I know first hand how this concept works. Here are some of my thoughts on the three time frames we understand as the past, present, and future.

The Past

Our past management decisions created our present. The major value of the past is what it can teach us. The past often screams at us with wisdom that we ignore. It usually takes significant reflection to get these lessons. Such lessons are essentially free today—we paid the price already. Repeating the mistakes of the past will doom our clients, associates, shareholders, and the Cerner enterprise. Repeating the things we know work, will position us to thrive. The one caveat: the future is never the analogue of the past. As a manager, you are responsible for anticipating the changes in our business and planning for them.

The Present

The present commands our attention; it is what is in our windshield. It is tomorrow's past. It was yesterday's future. It is a function of numerous decisions that were made weeks, months, and years ago, made real today. A wise manager contemplates the present as the result of choices, not accidents.

The Future

The future will get here, and probably much sooner than you expect. As a manager, I can change only the future. The past has been etched. The present is writing itself with a velocity that is difficult to bend. Now is a function of the quality of decisions that have been made to date. *The future, however, can be changed in the present.* My job as a manager is to create the future. The only way for me to accomplish this is to spend some quality time working on it. This has always been the most exciting part of management to me. Hopefully you see it throughout this book. Start with vision. Work top-down, bottom-up. Plan *i*T. Make it a habit to THINK.

As the chairman and chief executive officer, I clearly accept the responsibility for creating the future for Cerner. But the reality is that every manager at Cerner has the same responsibility. The biggest difference is the scope of our responsibilities and decisions. As CEO, I accept the responsibility for Cerner's future three, five, and even ten years out. I realize that if these trees are not planted today and nurtured, we are at risk as a company when that future becomes our present. If you are the managing director of *PathNet* (a role I have played) then you are responsible for where *PathNet* will be three, five, and even ten years out. If you manage Cerner Properties in Kansas City during the Midwestern heat wave, you must have a plan for how to clear the streets when we get the 10-inch Midwestern snowstorm.

NEAL PATTERSON

Clients will almost never tell you to invest, or where to invest, for the future. The client will say, just fix my present, be good at what you are. As a manager, you must have empathy with the client and deliver quality solutions, but you also must balance present needs with future investments. Imagining and investing in the future are the root of innovation, and innovation is, over the long term, the thing that keeps Cerner relevant in the eyes of our clients.

Most managers are consumed with the present. It is understandable. They have their hands on the wheel and are driving demanding, curving roads. A lot is hitting the windshield. Without a great deal of attention, our vehicle (Cerner) ends up in a ditch. Worse yet, we propel ourselves over some big cliff. I hate it when that happens. The really high-quality managers know how to abstract themselves from the present and envision a very different tomorrow. They have the discipline to plant a tree today.

The Enemy of *Good* Is *Perfect*

I have already said that I admired John F. Kennedy for articulating one of the boldest visions in the last half of the last century. I also learned a valuable lesson from the way the vision was accomplished.

To realize JFK's vision of sending a man to the moon, numerous inventions and innovations were required. One of these was the ability to sight a moving target that was extremely far away. This had never been done before. The conclusion was reached that there was no need for extreme precision in calculating the trajectory of the space vehicle at the outset. The most important thing would be to start in generally the right direction and recalculate the flight path as the ship got closer to the target and more information was available. The result was that, to get to the moon, the vehicle would follow a zigzag flight path. Precision was not important during most of the flight. The lesson: *You are never on the correct path, and you must always recalculate your direction.*

I have found this to be very important in accomplishing big things. It also relates to my desire to get started. If you invest all available time in optimizing the initial plan, you never start.

The manager who attempts to optimize at the expense of continuously adjusting and improving is failing. I have never felt smart enough to optimize, or solve a large problem once and for all, given the number of independent variables that are typically in motion in our environment. Get to *good*, and then pull the trigger.

Jump When the Window Is Open

I learned an important concept, *When the window is open, jump through it*, from one of the original members of Cerner's Board of Directors, Jim Jackson. To build the context requires a bit of storytelling from the early days of Cerner (or in this case, PGI).

We raised our first round of venture funds in November 1983. The venture investment firm was the SBIC of First Chicago Bank, which was one of the largest venture capital investors at that time. The rest of the investors were smaller, local individuals. One of the byproducts of raising outside capital was the need to create our first real Board of Directors. Paul Flanigan from First Chicago was the venture capital firm's representative on the Board. Of course, Paul Gorup, Cliff Illig, and I were members. We asked Terry Dolan, M.D., our first client, to be a member. Jim Jackson, our largest local investor, was a natural choice to round out the group.

Jim was one of the best Board members we have ever had, and certainly one of the most colorful. He had turned entrepreneur after the age of 50, founding what would become a successful real estate company called Electronic Realty Associates (ERA). He sold the company in the late 1970s for cash (big cash) and turned investor. At Board meetings, he would pull his Rolls-Royce up to the front door and park it. From the beginning, Jim clearly saw the potential of Cerner, probably more clearly than I did at the time. He was approaching his 70s when we met, and I was probably 32. Although we never discussed this, he clearly chose to mentor me—one entrepreneur to another. I learned a lot from Jim.

Going public is a very big deal for any company. Whether to go public or remain private was an important decision that the Board of Directors had to make. We made that decision at a Board meeting in the summer of 1986. There was quite a bit of discussion, back and forth, pros and cons. The reality was that Cerner was not ready to go public in 1986. We had a good discussion at the meeting. Jim usually would carefully choose his time to participate in our discussions, letting others vet the subject before he would speak. When Jim spoke, we all listened. His advice was usually sage and profound.

Jim said, *"When the window is open, jump through it."* He went on to explain that, in business, you never know what the future will present to you. In his opinion, the window of opportunity was open at that moment in time for Cerner to become a public company. It did not matter to him that we were probably one to two years away from being as ready as we wanted to be. That is an eternity in the stock market. We went public in December 1986. The stock market crash of September 1987 was the worst crash since the Great Depression and completely closed out the IPO market for several years. The capital we gained from going public in late 1986 allowed us to expand beyond the clinical laboratory and create the first version of *Health Network Architecture*. I have used Jim's advice ever since.

The *Ah* Moments

I have found that I have two types of *Ah* moments: *Aha!* and *Ah, hell.*

I love the *Aha!* moment. It is the time when dots connect in my mind, and I feel my understanding of something move to the next level. It is a wonderful, brief moment in time when I get it. The big ones become flash moments in which I burn into memory the context surrounding the moment.

I described my concept of *Aha!* moments in a speech I gave to a group of regional entrepreneurs. Lamar Hunt, a world-class entrepreneur, was in the audience. Lamar gave a talk to the same group the next day and referenced my comments by recalling his own *Aha!* moment that led him to start the American Football League. At the age of 26, he was trying to buy an existing NFL team and move it to Dallas, which at the time had no team. He had spent months talking to several teams, with no success. He had tried to get the NFL to let him have a new franchise for Dallas, again with no success. On a trip back from Chicago, on the plane, it struck him. Baseball had both an American and a National league, so why couldn't football? He would simply start a new professional football league—the American Football League—and he would take the Dallas franchise personally. He proceeded to do just that in 1959, becoming the owner of the AFL's Dallas Texans. The NFL did not like his idea and immediately started a new franchise called the Dallas Cowboys. The rest is history. The Texans are that little team that now plays under a different name at Arrowhead in Kansas City. He said that, to this day, he can recall the entire context of that *Aha!* moment, including his seat number on the plane.

I recall the moment in 1992 when I understood how to close the loop in healthcare. This *Aha!* was the basis of the Cerner vision now known as the Community Health Model. I, too, was on an airplane, sitting in coach in a window seat on the port (left) side of the cabin. Unlike Lamar Hunt, I do not remember the seat number. The *Aha!* was just as clear, however. By closing the loop, healthcare would become a perpetually improving system, and every event would become a learning event. Whereas *HNA Classic* had been based on a patient inside a healthcare enterprise, our next architecture would be based on the person. It would require building a person-centric architecture, connecting the person in the home, structuring a common nomenclature into the architecture, and storing the empirical evidence in major data warehouses.

A new calm set in because I knew what we had to do as Cerner. The knowledge that it might take decades to accomplish it did not bother me; in fact, it took another 18 months to start *HNA Millennium*. Knowing our destination in our next phase as a company, however, was what drove me from that point forward. Aha! moments are like candy; they give you a temporary lift. You feel great for a while because you have unraveled some complexity in your mind. Then the high burns off and you go back to work, but your world is never the same as it was before.

I have another type of *Ah* moment, one that I do not enjoy having. I call it an *Ah, hell* moment. (I have to admit that often I use a cruder but more heartfelt expression, *Ah, s_ _ t.*) That is the moment when I realize we have made a major mistake or are facing a huge unsolved problem. It is a moment for which I have conditioned myself to get calm, because I know that we will need to make some very big and quick decisions to fix the problem. Somehow we blew the "art is in the timing" lesson. Now we may only get one more attempt to fix it because we have used all available time.

CHAPTER SEVEN

I sometimes think I have had too much experience with the *Ah, hell* moments, but they are a fact of life. One of the largest *Ah, hell* moments I have ever had was in March 1996. Cerner had great success during the period of 1992 through 1995 selling our integrated solutions (*HNA Classic*) to hospitals and medical centers. We had what was clearly the most coherent architecture for a healthcare organization in the world, and we were very successful with it. CERN was one of the hottest stocks on Wall Street, and we had split our stock three times during that period. Then, in 1994, I committed Cerner to the path of building *HNA Millennium*. By 1996, we were well on the way, but the really rough part of the road was immediately ahead of us. I felt compelled to warn everyone at Cerner about what lay ahead, and, through a series of Town Hall meetings, I told Cerner associates in advance that 1996 was going to be one of the roughest years Cerner had ever experienced.

During that period of time, we created our financial and operating plans for Cerner offset from our fiscal year by one quarter. Our senior executive team had been working on the 1996 annual plan for months. I kept asking to see it. I remember everyone was so proud of the new tools they were using to prepare the plan.

I had called for a Think Week in March 1996 and was going to use the week to cover a number of strategic subjects. You could feel the amount of activity in our industry. Our clients were all consolidating into health systems, meaning they were trying to vertically integrate health plans, physician practices, hospitals, and home health into a single organization. Our competitors were trying to dominate our industry through a highly touted roll-up acquisition strategy, especially HBOC. They had captured Wall Street's attention and were viciously competing against Cerner in the marketplace. This was an extremely important time for Cerner, and I wanted to make sure that the windshield effect did not keep us from some deeper thinking. I decided to take a core team of senior managers to one of my favorite Missouri destinations, Big Cedar Lodge at Table Rock Lake (a great place—take the family). Each day, another group would come down, and our core team would go deep into their area. The week was going great. We had made progress on a number of important subjects.

Every evening, we would have dinner with both the team of executives that had been there for the day and the incoming team for the next day. Roughly in the middle of the week, at dinner, one of the executives that had just arrived gave me an envelope addressed to me, marked highly confidential. At the dinner table, I quietly opened and read the letter to myself. It was from Charlie McCall, chairman and CEO of HBOC. It was an offer to buy Cerner—the start of what we had to assume would be an attempt at a hostile takeover of Cerner. I calmly passed it to Cliff. He read it and passed it back. I put it in my pocket and enjoyed the evening.

The topic of the next day was financial operations. In that day, I was to get my first review of the highly anticipated 1996 financial plan. Intentionally, I scheduled this for the last topic of the day, so that we could focus on more strategic subjects before dealing with the plan. In parallel with the day's activities, Cliff and I notified our outside attorney of the letter and started what I knew would be a painful, expensive process of keeping our company independent.

It was around 6:00 P.M. before I got to see the plan. I was given the summary. I did not believe what I was seeing. I tested my understanding by asking some questions. For a brief moment, I thought that the team was joking with me. I had spent the previous two months telling the entire company just how difficult the next several years were going to be for Cerner. NONE of this was represented in the plan. The senior team had just assumed that the trends of the past three years would continue. They were using a ruler to predict the future.

In essence, at that moment, we had no real plan. We were under attack by the most aggressive competitor in the industry. I knew McCall personally. He was a very smart guy. He knew as well as I that HBOC had no architecture comparable to Cerner's supporting them, but they had great momentum. Much of the industry thought they had won. Buying Cerner would fix his problems. And he had caught us at one of our weakest moments.

It was a true *Ah, s_ _t* moment for me. This was no joke. It was all very real. Cerner was at risk. Any wrong move and we were gone. We had wasted valuable time.

It seemed like all of this happened in a single moment. I caught myself being mad. I vented for a moment. About that time, the group of executives for the next day's topics showed up, excited to be there and part of the process. I told them I was sorry, but they would have to go home. I had only one thing to do: build a plan. I formed a team of three and told everyone else to go home. I went down to the dock and watched the sun set. (Remember, the first step is to get calm—nothing better than sunsets.) Afterwards, I came back up and the three of us worked around the clock for two weeks to build the plan that I had assumed the senior executives had been building over the previous three months.

The *Ah* moments can be good *or* bad moments when you realize a change in direction is needed. Ultimately, they are about trusting yourself, even when it requires difficult action as a result.

****

These are my pearls. It is my hope that in them, you find some jewels for your collection.

Conclusion

I told you at the outset that I am no master of management, but still I wrote this book. Why? It's quite simple. As your manager, I felt a responsibility to convey my expectations and thoughts to you regarding your role as one of Cerner's managers. My method in this book has been to share with you some things that have been of great value to me. I have had 25-plus years to learn from my own experiences and to watch other managers up close. In writing this, I am simply moving the thoughts and observations out of my head and into the minds of people who are doing the work. I believe that *to grow*—as individuals, as a group, and as a species—is *to learn* from each other, to make the leap of internalizing experiences we've never personally had. I define a smart person as one who learns from their own mistakes and a wise person as one who learns from mistakes made by others. I don't want you to become me; I want you to surpass me.

Will you make some mistakes on your way? A given. There will be times when your plans go awry, your decisions prove wrong. There will be occasions when another style might have worked better. Sometimes you will think you understood the facts, only to find out that you didn't. There may even be times when you fail due to your own judgment. You will be justly criticized for your mistakes, and other times you will be criticized when you are doing the right thing. Your biggest mistakes will come when you fail to make decisions. Your biggest silent challenge will be your ethics—making the right decision in the face of tremendous pressures to do otherwise.

To be a manager is to commit yourself to a level of scrutiny and risk that nonmanagers do not endure. You must accept the responsibility for the inherent quality, productivity, and profitability of your part of the organization. You are accountable to your team, your peers, our clients, and our shareholders to deliver results on time. You will get no credit for effort. Most of the time you will not get noticed for doing your job.

If you do not want your faults and weaknesses to be exposed, if you do not want to be judged by others above and below, if you are fearful of making choices that will impact other people, if you are driven by a strong need to be liked by others, or if you can't bear the idea that your decisions will be weighed against a thousand imaginary alternates, you shouldn't be a manager.

If, on the other hand, you accept the fact that you will operate and be judged in a state of perpetual ambiguity; if you can still actively *plan, execute,* and *control* in the face of past mistakes, present pressures, and future uncertainty; if you have committed yourself not to perfection but to continuous learning and improvement; and if you find that, when all is said and done, you are still exhilarated by making decisions that shape healthcare, our communities, the enterprise called Cerner, and its clients, associates, and shareholders—in other words, if you can *Manage*—you will do well for yourself and for Cerner. Your decisions, actions, and results will create *i*T— our future. Managers manage.

Neal ...

Index